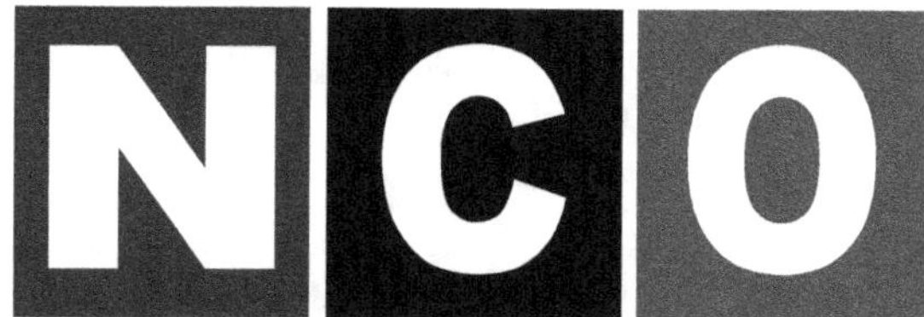

OLYMPIAD WORKBOOK

NATIONAL CYBER OLYMPIAD

01 Learning Objectives

02 Multiple Choice Questions

03 HOTS (Achievers Section)

04 Model Test Paper

05 Answer Keys and Solutions

06 OMR Answer Sheet

V&S PUBLISHERS

Published by:

V&S PUBLISHERS

F-2/16, Ansari road, Daryaganj, New Delhi-110002
☎ 23240026, 23240027 • *Fax:* 011-23240028
✉ info@vspublishers.com • 🌐 www.vspublishers.com

Online Brandstore: amazon.in/vspublishers

Regional Office : Hyderabad
5-1-707/1, Brij Bhawan (Beside Central Bank of India Lane)
Bank Street, Koti, Hyderabad - 500 095
☎ 040-24737290
✉ vspublishershyd@gmail.com

Follow us on:   

BUY OUR BOOKS FROM: AMAZON | FLIPKART

© **Copyright:** *V&S PUBLISHERS*
ISBN 978-81-978176-1-8
New Edition

DISCLAIMER

While every attempt has been made to provide accurate and timely information in this book, neither the author nor the publisher assumes any responsibility for errors, unintended omissions or commissions detected therein. The author and publisher makes no representation or warranty with respect to the comprehensiveness or completeness of the contents provided.

All matters included have been simplified under professional guidance for general information only, without any warranty for applicability on an individual. Any mention of an organization or a website in the book, by way of citation or as a source of additional information, doesn't imply the endorsement of the content either by the author or the publisher. It is possible that websites cited may have changed or removed between the time of editing and publishing the book.

Results from using the expert opinion in this book will be totally dependent on individual circumstances and factors beyond the control of the author and the publisher.

It makes sense to elicit advice from well informed sources before implementing the ideas given in the book. The reader assumes full responsibility for the consequences arising out from reading this book.

For proper guidance, it is advisable to read the book under the watchful eyes of parents/guardian. The buyer of this book assumes all responsibility for the use of given materials and information.

The copyright of the entire content of this book rests with the author/publisher. Any infringement/transmission of the cover design, text or illustrations, in any form, by any means, by any entity will invite legal action and be responsible for consequences thereon.

PUBLISHER'S NOTE

V&S Publishers has carved a significant niche in the publishing industry over the last decade, having successfully published more than 1000 titles across 9 languages spanning over 50 subject categories. Being known for the quality of content, we have built a reputation of excellence and reliability. We have consistently delivered **"Value & Substance"** to our readers, through a wide range of titles across a variety of genres covering school books, fiction and non-fiction that caters to different people from every section of the society.

The **Olympiad Guidebooks for classes 1-10** across all subjects, launched almost a decade ago, under the **GEN X Imprint**, became a go-to-source for the school students in no time, owing to their invaluable and substantive content written in a guidebook pattern,.

Having successfully sold a million copies of the same and in response to demand by both students as well as shopkeepers nationwide; we now present before you our newly launched **Olympiad Workbook Series**, designed for **classes 1-10 across 4 subjects**.

The workbooks are meticulously curated by a team of experienced educators, researchers and subject matter experts, edited by professionals and peer reviewed by teachers. The team has poured its efforts and expertise into creating a crisp and concise workbook which will help and guide the students to the path of success in Olympiad exams. The **MCQs** identified will not only help in scoring top marks in Olympiads but also inculcate a sense of deeper understanding of the subject, by way of solving **HOTS** and referring to complete solutions at the end of the book.

Here we present our new release– **OLYMPIAD WORKBOOK (NCO) CLASS–2** having following features:

- ☞ Based on the latest syllabi
- ☞ MCQs with comprehensive coverage of topics
- ☞ HOTS Questions liberally included
- ☞ A dedicated chapter on logical reasoning
- ☞ Model test paper for thorough practice
- ☞ Sample OMR sheet for real time simulation

We have made sure through our best efforts, that this workbook strictly follows the latest syllabi and patterns of the Olympiad Examination.

As **V&S Publishers** continuously strive to enhance the readability and maintain the credibility of our academic publications, we seek the support of our valuable readers in influencing and enriching the lives of future generations of students.

P.S. While every care has been taken to ensure the correctness of the content, if you come across any error, howsoever minor, do not hesitate to discuss with teachers while pointing that out to us in no uncertain terms.

We wish you all the best for your exams!

DISTINCTIVE FEATURES

01 Learning Objectives

They list the whole chapter as subtopics, helping the teachers to guide children in a step-by-step manner.

02 Multiple Choice Questions

MCQs act as an excellent learning aid, helping you to understand and work on your mistakes.

03 HOTS (Achievers Section)

The High Order Thinking Questions aim to help the student to solve Application-based questions and gain practical understanding of the subject.

04 Model Test Paper

Model test paper are provided at the end of each book, which help the student to test the knowledge which they have gained after thorough reading of all chapters.

05 Answer Key

Detailed Answer Key along with explanations aid the pupil to indentify, understand the mistakes they make during the course of Olympiad preparation.

CONTENTS

INTRODUCTION TO COMPUTER

LEARNING OBJECTIVES

➤ What is a Computer?
➤ Types of Computers
➤ Computer Versus Man

MULTIPLE CHOICE QUESTIONS

1. Which is the most powerful in terms of memory?
   (A) Desktop
   (B) Palmtop
   (C) Tablet
   (D) Mainframe computer

2. Which computer has the smallest screen?

   (A) 
   Tablet

   (B) 
   Desktop

   (C) 
   Laptop

   (D) 
   Mainframe computer

3. Which task cannot be performed by a computer?
   (A) Drawing images
   (B) Writing letters
   (C) Illuminating a room
   (D) Calculating sums

4. Find the odd one out.

   (A) 
   Palmtop

   (B) 
   Laptop

   (C) 
   Calculator

   (D) 
   Washing Machine

5. A computer cannot
   (A) Work tirelessly
   (B) Remember everything
   (C) Run fast
   (D) Calculate fast

6. Unjumble the word and find out which is not a type of computer.
   (A) PLAOTP
   (B) DSPTKEO
   (C) TLVISOEEIN
   (D) BTTLEA

7. This is not an electronic machine.

   (A) 
   Bicycle

   (B) 
   Microwave

   (C) 
   Mobile phone

   (D) 
   Laptop

8. This abbreviation does not relate to computers.
   (A) VDU
   (B) ALU
   (C) BSc
   (D) Kb

9. Tick the place where we do not see a computer.
   (A) Superstore
   (B) Airport
   (C) Temple
   (D) Drawing room

10. This feature is uncommon between a man and a computer.
   (A) Memory
   (B) Calculation
   (C) Voice
   (D) Emotions

11. Which computer type is best suited for an airport?

   (A) 
   Laptop

   (B) 
   Mainframe computer

   (C) 
   Desktop

   (D) 
   Supercomputer

12. Ravi is a class 2 student. Which type of computer should he use to learn the basic functioning of a computer?
   (A) Supercomputer   (B) Laptop
   (C) Desktop   (D) Tablet

13. Which type of computer has a touch screen?
    (A) Palmtop   (B) Tablet
    (C) Laptop   (D) All of them

14. We find several punching keys on the
    (A) Washing machine
    (B) Calculator
    (C) Desktop
    (D) (B) and (C) both

15. A computer cannot search
    (A) Lost file
    (B) Lost image
    (C) Lost key
    (D) Lost document

16. While working on a computer, we should not
    (A) work in bright light
    (B) keep the computer clean
    (C) sit straight
    (D) bend forward towards the screen

17. Which is the best statement to define a computer?
    (A) A computer is a man-made electronic device.
    (B) A computer is a man-made electronic device that can store a lot of data.
    (C) A computer is an electronic device.
    (D) A computer is a smart device.

18. This cannot be a computer game.
    (A) Car race
    (B) Creative art
    (C) Bike race
    (D) Hide-N-Seek

19. This computer has several wires.
    (A) Laptop
    (B) Mainframe computer
    (C) Desktop
    (D) Tablet

20. This term is not related to computers.
    (A) Speed   (B) Memory
    (C) Fatigue   (D) File

HOTS (ACHIEVERS SECTION)

21. Which option will process this information faster?

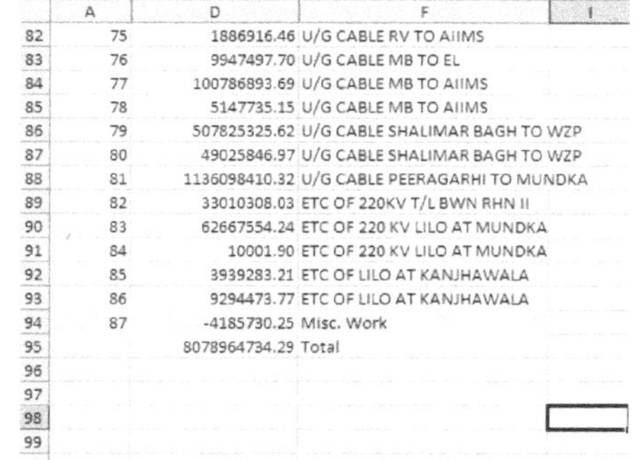

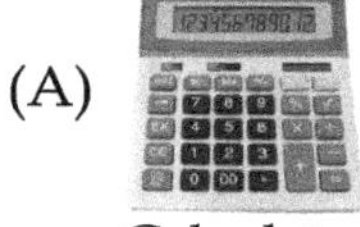

(A) Calculator

(B) Computer

(C) Paper pen

(D) Typewriter

22. Identify the devices marked as X and Y with the help of given information.

Device X	Device Y
It is not portable.	It comes with a touchpad.

(A) Device X -    Device Y - 

(B) Device X -    Device Y - 

(C) Device X -    Device Y - 

(D) Device X -    Device Y - 

23. Select the hand-held device that can be connected with the desktop computer using a wire (known as data cable).

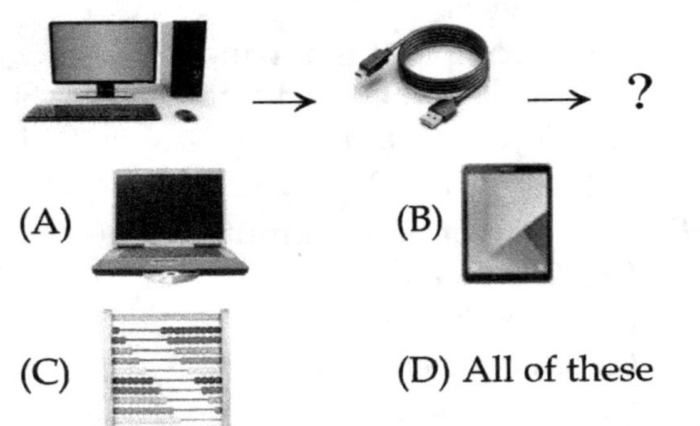

(A)

(B)

(C)

(D) All of these

24. To which location does a deleted file is stored when we DELETE a file?

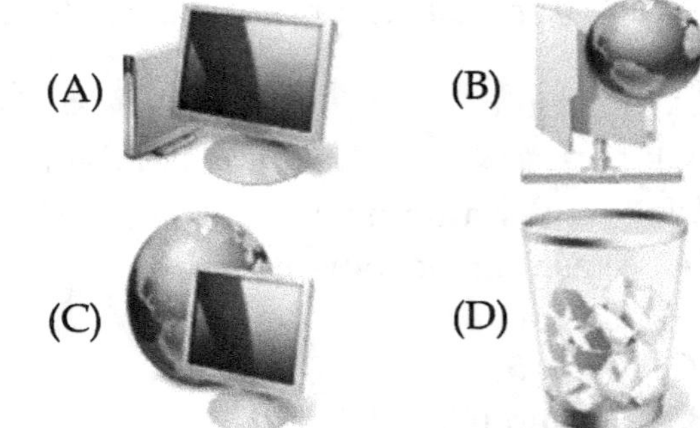

(A)

(B)

(C)

(D)

25. Speed of Laser Printer is measured in which unit?
(A) LPM (B) DPS
(C) DPI (D) PPM

1.	Ⓐ Ⓑ Ⓒ Ⓓ	6.	Ⓐ Ⓑ Ⓒ Ⓓ	11.	Ⓐ Ⓑ Ⓒ Ⓓ	16.	Ⓐ Ⓑ Ⓒ Ⓓ	21.	Ⓐ Ⓑ Ⓒ Ⓓ
2.	Ⓐ Ⓑ Ⓒ Ⓓ	7.	Ⓐ Ⓑ Ⓒ Ⓓ	12.	Ⓐ Ⓑ Ⓒ Ⓓ	17.	Ⓐ Ⓑ Ⓒ Ⓓ	22.	Ⓐ Ⓑ Ⓒ Ⓓ
3.	Ⓐ Ⓑ Ⓒ Ⓓ	8.	Ⓐ Ⓑ Ⓒ Ⓓ	13.	Ⓐ Ⓑ Ⓒ Ⓓ	18.	Ⓐ Ⓑ Ⓒ Ⓓ	23.	Ⓐ Ⓑ Ⓒ Ⓓ
4.	Ⓐ Ⓑ Ⓒ Ⓓ	9.	Ⓐ Ⓑ Ⓒ Ⓓ	14.	Ⓐ Ⓑ Ⓒ Ⓓ	19.	Ⓐ Ⓑ Ⓒ Ⓓ	24.	Ⓐ Ⓑ Ⓒ Ⓓ
5.	Ⓐ Ⓑ Ⓒ Ⓓ	10.	Ⓐ Ⓑ Ⓒ Ⓓ	15.	Ⓐ Ⓑ Ⓒ Ⓓ	20.	Ⓐ Ⓑ Ⓒ Ⓓ	25.	Ⓐ Ⓑ Ⓒ Ⓓ

OLYMPIAD WORKBOOK (NCO) CLASS – 2

FUNDAMENTALS OF COMPUTER

LEARNING OBJECTIVES

➤ Starting a Computer
➤ Shutting Down a Computer
➤ IPO Cycle
➤ General Information on Computer

MULTIPLE CHOICE QUESTIONS

1. Find the odd one out.
   (A) Power   (B) Toggle
   (C) Switch   (D) Goggle

2. UPS, CPU, monitor, keyboard and all other computer devices are connected with
   (A) Power button   (B) Wires
   (C) Chips   (D) Magnets

3. The first calculating device was
   (A) Calculator   (B) Typewriter
   (C) Desktop   (D) Abacus

4. Icons are present on the
   (A) Desktop main screen
   (B) Taskbar
   (C) System tray
   (D) All of them

5. The following icon is of:

   (A) System tray   (B) Folder
   (C) File   (D) Software

6. Look at the image below and write what command will lead you to this:

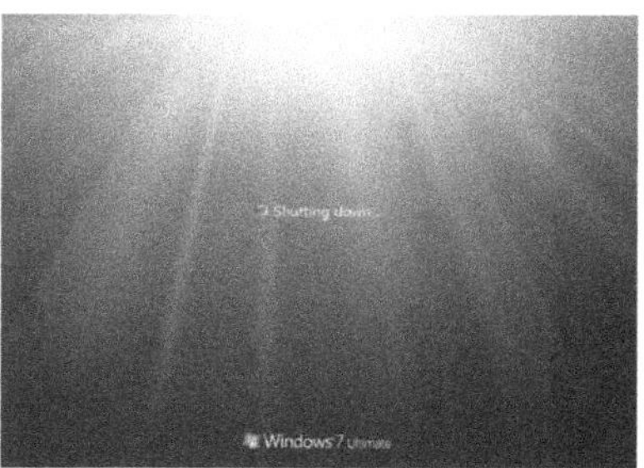

   (A) Ctrl+ALT+Del
   (B) Start button → Shut down
   (C) Start button → Hibernate
   (D) CTRL+Del

7. What does this icon mean on the desktop?

   (A) An icon
   (B) A software

(C) A hardware

(D) A mouse pointer

8. This is the unit for memory.

(A) Byte   (B) Hertz

(C) Metre   (D) Kilogram

9. Pixel is related to which part of the computer?

(A) Keyboard   (B) CPU

(C) Monitor   (D) UPS

10. UPS stands for

(A) Uninterrupted power supply

(B) Unhindered power supply

(C) Unwanted power supply

(D) Unique power supply

11. Observe the sequence below. Which option follows the IPO cycle?

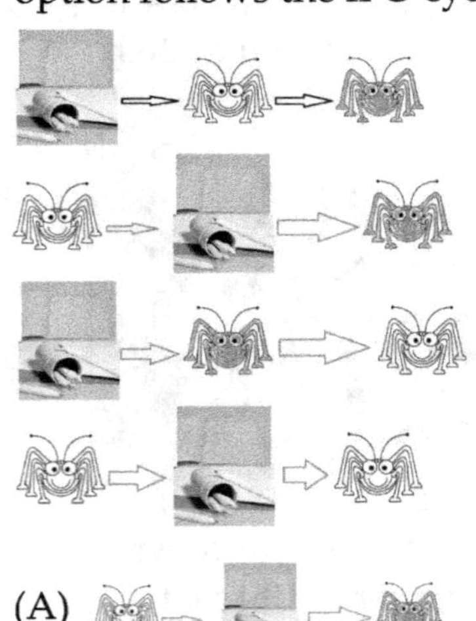

(A) 

(B) 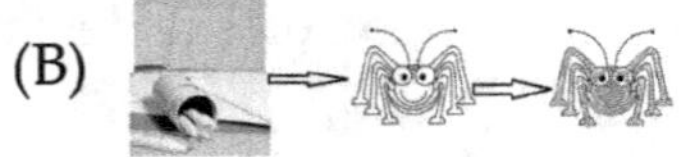

(C) 

(D) 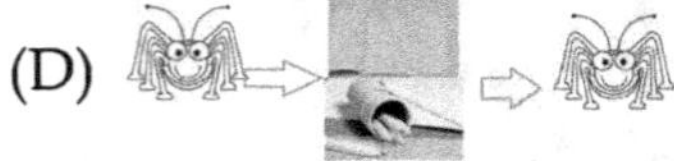

12. Which option is correctly matched?

(A) Monitor-Input; Printer-Output; CPU-Process

(B) Keyboard-Input; CPU-process; Monitor-Output

(C) Mouse-Input; CPU-Process; Keyboard-Output

(D) Mouse-Input; CPU-Process and Output

13. In the image given below, what are X, Y and Z?

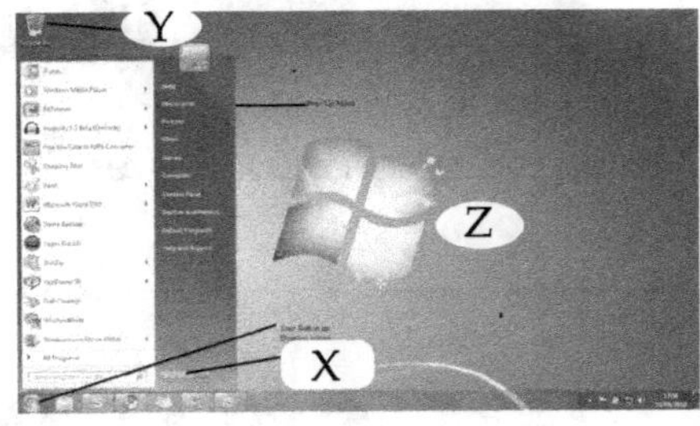

	X	Y	Z
(A)	Switch off	Boot button	Screensaver button
(B)	Start Button	Icon	Wallpaper
(C)	Shut Down Button	Icon	Desktop Screen
(D)	Icon	Boot Button	Wallpaper

14. The time taken by a CPU to ready itself for functioning is called

(A) Cold Boot   (B) Warm Boot

(C) Hibernate   (D) Start up

15. 'Switching ON' of the power switch is called

(A) Start Up

(B) Switch User

(C) Cold Boot

(D) Warm Boot

16. The area of desktop that displays the time

(A) Taskbar

(B) System Tray

(C) Icon

(D) Pop-up Menu

OLYMPIAD WORKBOOK (NCO) CLASS – 2

17. Name the language understood by a computer.
    (A) Binary digits: Machine language
    (B) Alphabets
    (C) Numeric
    (D) Tertiary digits: Machine language
18. Which can be a code related to computer language?
    (A) A1001A
    (B) 101010
    (C) 1016101017
    (D) FGFTDRRFV
19. What is ALU and what is its location?

	I	II
(A)	Arithmetic Logical Unit	Monitor
(B)	Arithmetic Logic Unit	CPU
(C)	Arithmetic Language	CPU
(D)	Arithmetic Logic Unit	Keyboard

20. This cannot be an input device.

(A) 
Keyboard

(B)
Mouse

(C)
Laptop Touchpad

(D)
Printer

HOTS (ACHIEVERS SECTION)

21. Ravi's father suffered from severe backache, his doctor recommended him not to use the computer, what could be the possible reason?
    I.   He worked for long hours on the computer.
    II. He did not sit properly while working on the computer.
    III. He played games on computers.
    (A) I and II
    (B) I and III
    (C) I
    (D) II
22. Mr A and Mr B are neighbours. They both work on computers the whole day. They use the same electrical gadgets. But Mr. A's computer battery drains faster than Mr. B's. Why?
    I.   Electric cuts are more in Mr. B's house.
    II. Mr. A does not 'hibernate' the computer when not in use.
    III. Mr B 'hibernates' the computer when not in use.
    IV. Mr. A's computer battery may be old.
    (A) I, II and III
    (B) I and III
    (C) II, III and IV
    (D) III and IV
23. A group of 5 students were trying some codes. Identify which student can directly relate his/her code to computer language.

Student name	Code
Chang	ag6t21bi9hydxnb
John	FGTUYFFTUYIK
Lily	10101011111
Tina	0001100000
Sam	O)O)OHUGF^CD$%

(A) Tina and Sam
(B) John and Lily
(C) Lily and Sam
(D) Lily and Tina

24. Which of the following shows the CORRECT order of IPO cycle?

(A) 

(B)

(C)

(D) All of these

25. In the given image, box marked as 'X' requires the secret series of characters in order to have access to the computer. This secret series of characters is known as ______.

(A) Password
(B) Wallpaper
(C) Context
(D) Tools

PARTS OF A COMPUTER

3

➤ Input Devices
➤ Processing DeviceS
➤ Storage Devices
➤ Output Devices

MULTIPLE CHOICE QUESTIONS

1. Look at the desktop image below and find out which part is labelled incorrectly.

(A) Monitor   (B) Keyboard
(C) Speakers   (D) Mouse

2. This is not an input device.

(A) 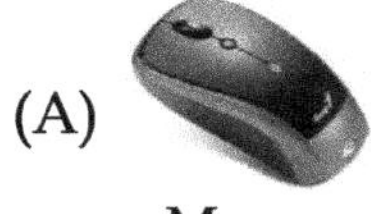
Mouse

(B) 
Monitor

(C) 
Keyboard

(D) 
Trackball

3. This is an input device.

(A) 
Elephant

(B) 
Snake

(C) 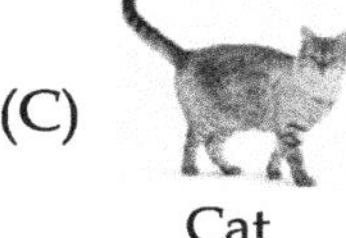
Cat

(D) 
Mouse

4. This produces musical sound.

(A) 
Web camera

(B) 
Printer

(C) 
Scanner

(D) 
Speaker

5. This is not an essential part of a desktop.

(A) 
Web camera

(B) 
Mouse

(C) 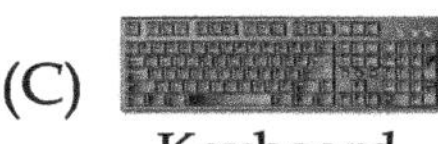
Keyboard

(D) 
Monitor

6. Observe the image below. What could it be?

(A) An input device
(B) An output device
(C) A storage device
(D) None of these

7. While playing a game, we use this the most.

(A) 
Mouse

(B) 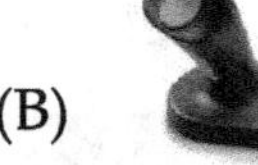
Joystick and mouse

(C) 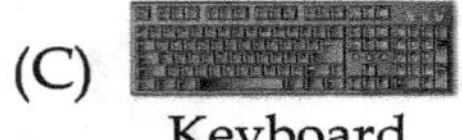
Keyboard

(D) 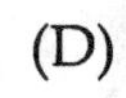
Scanner

8. This is not a storage device.

(A) 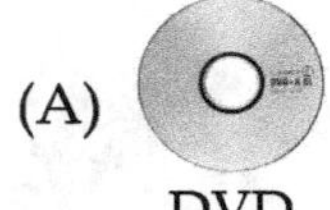
DVD

(B) 
Blu-ray

(C) 
Hard disc

(D) 
Scanner

9. We find !, @, %, ^ type of symbols on the

(A) 
Web camera

(B) 
Mouse

(C) 
Keyboard

(D) 
Monitor

10. This is the brain of the computer.

(A) 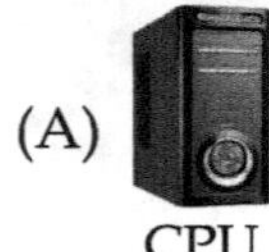
CPU

(B) 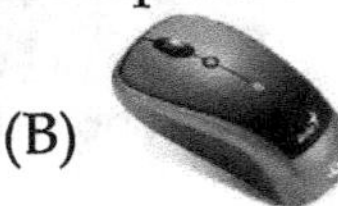
Mouse

(C) Keyboard

(D) 
Monitor

11. Match the following

I	II
(A) 	(i) CD
(B) 	(ii) Mouse
(C) 	(iii) Scanner
(D) 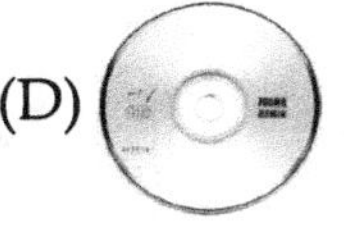	(iv) Hard disc

(A) a-i, b-ii, c-iii, d-iv
(B) a-ii, b-iii, c-iv, d-i
(C) a-iii, b-i, c-ii, d-iv
(D) a-iv, b-iii, c-ii, d-i

12. Observe the image below. What is it?

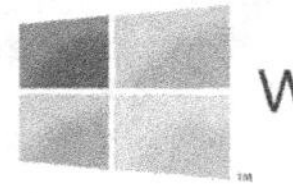

(A) Keyboard symbol
(B) Mouse pointer
(C) Desktop screen image
(D) Windows logo

13. It is a circular device which is not attached to the computer with a wire.
(A) Mouse
(B) Track ball
(C) DVD
(D) Web camera

14. This does not belong to the CPU.
(A) ALU   (B) CD
(C) CU   (D) Hard Disc

15. Meena wants to submit a project that she did on her computer, which device will she use?
(A) Scanner (B) Monitor
(C) Printer (D) Speaker

16. What is a scanner?
(A) A scanner is a device that transfers the picture kept on its surface to the computer.
(B) A scanner is a device that creates images.
(C) A scanner is a device that helps us to take printouts.
(D) A scanner is a sound-producing device.

17. We store a large amount of data in:

(A) 
Mouse

(B) 
Monitor

(C) 
Blu-ray

(D) 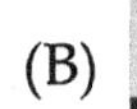
CPU

18. To watch a movie, which parts of a computer will you use?
(A) Monitor, Speaker, CPU
(B) Monitor
(C) Printer
(D) CPU

19. I am a unique device. I help you to communicate with others through a computer.

(A) 
Microphone

(B) 
Scanner

(C) 
Web camera

(D) 
Headphones

20. Which device can store the highest amount of information?
(A) CPU
(B) DVD
(C) CD
(D) Blu-ray

HOTS (ACHIEVERS SECTION)

21. There was a grand fun fair going on in a city. A child got lost. The fun fair had computerised cameras installed all over. Which device will the security personnel use to search that child's parents?

(A) 

(B) 

(C) 

(D) 

22. With which computer parts does the following image correlate?

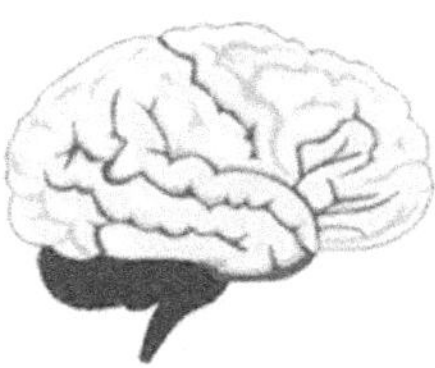

I.   Mouse   II. CD
III. Blu-Ray   IV. CPU
(A) IV   (B) I and II
(C) I   (D) III and IV

23. Which of the following is NOT a part of computer?

(A) 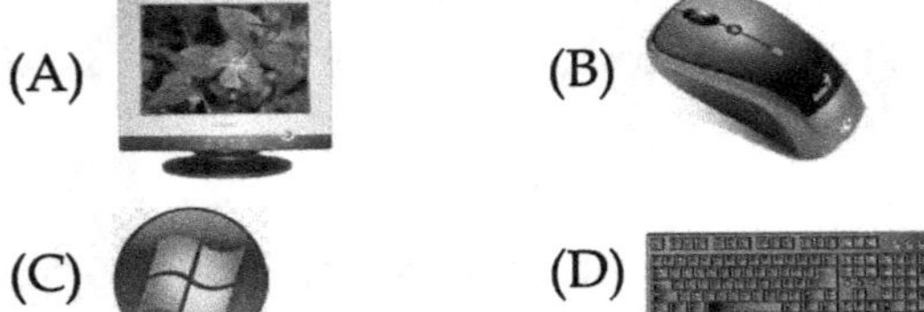

(B)

(C)

(D)

24. Which of the following states the CORRECT difference between the given two devices?

(A)		
	It is a pointing device.	It is not a pointing device.
(B)		
	It can be connected to the computer.	It cannot be connected to the computer.

(C)		
	It is used to give input to the computer.	It is used to display output to the computer.
(D)		
	It can be used to draw pictures on screen.	It cannot be used to draw pictures on screen.

25. Identify the external power supply unit given below that is used to plug the computer into a standard electrical outlet.

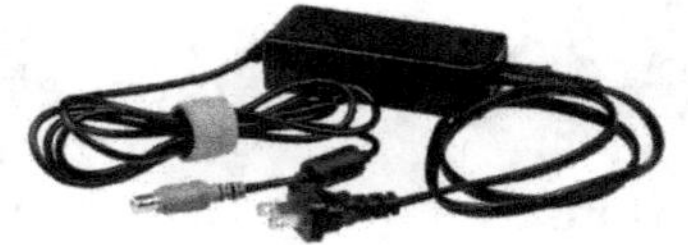

(A) Monitor   (B) USB Cable

(C) AC adapter   (D) Keyboard

Darken Your Choice with HB Pencil

1.	Ⓐ Ⓑ Ⓒ Ⓓ	6.	Ⓐ Ⓑ Ⓒ Ⓓ	11.	Ⓐ Ⓑ Ⓒ Ⓓ	16.	Ⓐ Ⓑ Ⓒ Ⓓ	21.	Ⓐ Ⓑ Ⓒ Ⓓ
2.	Ⓐ Ⓑ Ⓒ Ⓓ	7.	Ⓐ Ⓑ Ⓒ Ⓓ	12.	Ⓐ Ⓑ Ⓒ Ⓓ	17.	Ⓐ Ⓑ Ⓒ Ⓓ	22.	Ⓐ Ⓑ Ⓒ Ⓓ
3.	Ⓐ Ⓑ Ⓒ Ⓓ	8.	Ⓐ Ⓑ Ⓒ Ⓓ	13.	Ⓐ Ⓑ Ⓒ Ⓓ	18.	Ⓐ Ⓑ Ⓒ Ⓓ	23.	Ⓐ Ⓑ Ⓒ Ⓓ
4.	Ⓐ Ⓑ Ⓒ Ⓓ	9.	Ⓐ Ⓑ Ⓒ Ⓓ	14.	Ⓐ Ⓑ Ⓒ Ⓓ	19.	Ⓐ Ⓑ Ⓒ Ⓓ	24.	Ⓐ Ⓑ Ⓒ Ⓓ
5.	Ⓐ Ⓑ Ⓒ Ⓓ	10.	Ⓐ Ⓑ Ⓒ Ⓓ	15.	Ⓐ Ⓑ Ⓒ Ⓓ	20.	Ⓐ Ⓑ Ⓒ Ⓓ	25.	Ⓐ Ⓑ Ⓒ Ⓓ

OLYMPIAD WORKBOOK (NCO) CLASS – 2

USES OF COMPUTER 

LEARNING OBJECTIVES

- ➤ At Home
- ➤ At Market
- ➤ At Banks
- ➤ At Other Places
- ➤ At School
- ➤ At Hospitals

MULTIPLE CHOICE QUESTIONS

1. A school has computers at the following places
   - (A) Library
   - (B) Library and computer class
   - (C) Library, school office and computer class
   - (D) School office

2. At home we do not use computer for
   - (A) Playing games
   - (B) Washing clothes
   - (C) Making projects
   - (D) Watching movies

3. In a library, computers help in:
   - (A) Maintaining salary records
   - (B) Maintaining book records
   - (C) Maintaining students performance records
   - (D) Making test papers

4. In an office, computers

I. Make a task lengthy
II. Make employee attendance records
III. Make salary records
IV. Make working difficult

   - (A) I only
   - (B) II and III
   - (C) IV only
   - (D) I and IV

5. We find an ATM in
   - (A) A bank
   - (B) A space station
   - (C) An office
   - (D) A library

6. Philip is facing problems in deciding, which flight he should take to reach his brother's wedding on time. How will he get this information?
   - (A) Philip will call in a bank; flight schedules are maintained in a dairy
   - (B) Philip will call in a newspaper office; flight schedules are maintained in a newspaper
   - (C) Philip will call an airport officer; flight schedules are maintained in a computer
   - (D) Philip will call in a school library; flight schedules are maintained in a book

7. Which place is shown in the image below?

(A) A library   (B) A school
(C) An office   (D) A superstore

8. What is the person doing in the image shown below?

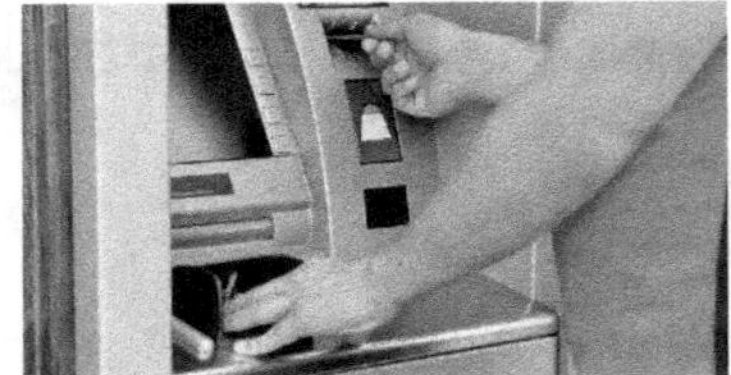

(A) Withdrawing money from an ATM
(B) Withdrawing money from a bank window
(C) Submitting a book in a library
(D) Taking out a ticket

9. In a space station, a computer
(A) Monitors satellite positions
(B) Monitors space activities and satellite positions
(C) Monitors weather changes, space activities and satellite positions
(D) Monitors flight schedules

10. Rehan has purchased lots of stuff from a shopping mall. What will the computer do now?
(A) A computer will give him discount.
(B) A computer will give him a certificate.
(C) A computer will generate a bill.
(D) A computer will give him money.

11. During the summer holidays, Saima and her friends went to a water park. At the water park they noticed computers. Tick the place where they could have seen computers:

(A) At the ticket counter
(B) At the swimming pool
(C) At the water ride
(D) In the costume room

12. Hemant has lost his library card. How could he find out the details?
(A) He can ask the school teacher.
(B) He can ask the librarian to check his computer data.
(C) He can ask his friends.
(D) He can ask his parents.

13. In a supermarket, there is a huge vegetable shop. The shop has 5 computers. What do the computers do there?

> (I) Keep vegetable stocks.
> (II) Keep vegetable price list
> (III) Keep customer name list
> (IV) Store vegetables

(A) I only
(B) III only
(C) I, II and III
(D) IV only

14. Which statement is true?
(A) In a space station, a computer prints books.
(B) In a school, a computer is used for playing games.
(C) In a bank, a computer is used to maintain money records.
(D) At home, computer is used to diagnose diseases.

15. In a hospital, where will you find a computer?
(A) In hospital office
(B) In the x-ray room
(C) In the laboratory
(D) All of the above

16. Which is not matched correctly?
(A) Office-record keeping
(B) Publishing-book designing

(C) Entertainment-games making

(D) Hospitals-watching movies

17. At an airport, what type of computer can we find?

(A) Laptop

(B) Desktop

(C) Desktop and Mainframe computer

(D) Tablets

18. Which of the following statements is incorrect for computers?

(A) Computers have reduced the time taken to withdraw money from a bank account.

(B) Computers have made learning an interesting process.

(C) Computers create boring games.

(D) Computers help in weather forecast.

19. In a village, we can find a computer at/in:

(A) A post office

(B) A bank

(C) A police station

(D) Every home

20. Who will not use a computer?

(A) a cyclist

(B) a pilot

(C) a metro train driver

(D) an astronaut

HOTS (ACHIEVERS SECTION)

21. Read the following statements. How many are true?

(I) Computers help maintain medicine stock records.

(II) Computers help in flying air planes.

(III) Computers help in running war tankers in war field.

(IV) Computers help in evaluating test sheets.

(A) I, II, III and IV

(B) I and II

(C) I and III

(D) I and IV

22. In Airlines and Railways computer are used for tickets. Which one of the following is correct about the another use of computer in airlines and Railway?

(A) Controlling the traffic

(B) Updating the time table

(C) Keeping records of passengers

(D) All of these

23. Consider the following statements:

Statement 1: Better keyboard skill gives best productivity.
Statement 2: The upper row of the keyboard contains function keys.
Statement 3: The keyboard contain 26 alphabets keys

Which one of the following is correct about the above statements?

(A) Statement 1 is true and 2 is false

(B) Statement 1 is true

(C) Statement 3 is true

(D) All are correct

(E) None of these

24. Marketing can be done over the internet. This is known as?

(A) e-banking

(B) e-marketing

(C) e-business

(D) e-books

25. Which device shown in the picture is used to project images from computer to a bigger screen?

(A) Projector
(B) Microphones
(C) Speakers
(D) Projector

1. Ⓐ Ⓑ Ⓒ Ⓓ	6. Ⓐ Ⓑ Ⓒ Ⓓ	11. Ⓐ Ⓑ Ⓒ Ⓓ	16. Ⓐ Ⓑ Ⓒ Ⓓ	21. Ⓐ Ⓑ Ⓒ Ⓓ
2. Ⓐ Ⓑ Ⓒ Ⓓ	7. Ⓐ Ⓑ Ⓒ Ⓓ	12. Ⓐ Ⓑ Ⓒ Ⓓ	17. Ⓐ Ⓑ Ⓒ Ⓓ	22. Ⓐ Ⓑ Ⓒ Ⓓ
3. Ⓐ Ⓑ Ⓒ Ⓓ	8. Ⓐ Ⓑ Ⓒ Ⓓ	13. Ⓐ Ⓑ Ⓒ Ⓓ	18. Ⓐ Ⓑ Ⓒ Ⓓ	23. Ⓐ Ⓑ Ⓒ Ⓓ
4. Ⓐ Ⓑ Ⓒ Ⓓ	9. Ⓐ Ⓑ Ⓒ Ⓓ	14. Ⓐ Ⓑ Ⓒ Ⓓ	19. Ⓐ Ⓑ Ⓒ Ⓓ	24. Ⓐ Ⓑ Ⓒ Ⓓ
5. Ⓐ Ⓑ Ⓒ Ⓓ	10. Ⓐ Ⓑ Ⓒ Ⓓ	15. Ⓐ Ⓑ Ⓒ Ⓓ	20. Ⓐ Ⓑ Ⓒ Ⓓ	25. Ⓐ Ⓑ Ⓒ Ⓓ

OLYMPIAD WORKBOOK (NCO) CLASS— 2

LEARNING TO USE KEYBOARD

LEARNING OBJECTIVES

- ➤ Alphabet Keys
- ➤ Symbol Keys
- ➤ Navigation
- ➤ Number Keys
- ➤ Function Keys
- ➤ Special Keys

MULTIPLE CHOICE QUESTIONS

1. Alphabet keys have
   (A) 1, 2, 3
   (B) B, T, g, a, s, D
   (C) @, $, ^, *,)
   (D) A, D, R, E, T

2. A shift key is used for
   (A) It is used to type numbers.
   (B) It is used in association with other keys to type symbols and capital letters.
   (C) It is used to type capital letters.
   (D) It is used to type symbols.

3. The number pad has the following series of numbers
   (A) 0-9
   (B) 1-10
   (C) 1-20
   (D) 1-100

4. Which set of keys is shown in the image below?

   F1 F2 F3 F4 F5 F6 F7 F8

   (A) Symbol
   (B) Alphabet
   (C) Number
   (D) Function

5. This is not a special key.
   (A) A, B, C
   (B) CTRL
   (C) Shift key
   (D) Alt

6. Read the statement below. Which key will you use to make the correction?
   An elephant is eating grass.
   (A) Home key
   (B) Backspace key
   (C) Delete key
   (D) Enter key

7. This is the longest key on the keyboard.
   (A) Enter
   (B) CTRL
   (C) Space bar
   (D) Function

8. Match the following correctly:

I	II
(i) Alphabet key	(a)
(ii) Shift key	(b)
(iii) Symbol Key	(c)
(iv) Function Key	(d)

(A) i-a, ii-b, iii-c, iv-d
(B) i-c, ii-d, iii-a, iv-b
(C) i-d, ii-c, iii-b, iv-a
(D) i-c, ii-a, iii-d, iv-b

9. An * will be typed with the help of
   (A) Shift key
   (B) Ctrl key
   (C) 8 no. key
   (D) Shift + 8

10. Rohit is on page 13 of a computer file, he wants to read a story on page 15. Which key will he use?
    (A) Backspace
    (B) Upward navigation key
    (C) Page Down
    (D) Page Up

11. Meena opened a program by mistake. She is unable to close it. What will she do?
    (A) She will press CTRL
    (B) She will press Esc
    (C) She will press Del
    (D) She will press Tab

12. A Caps Lock key of a keyboard is not functional. Which key would you use to type capital letters?
    (A) Shift key + Alphabet
    (B) Tab key + Alphabet
    (C) Number key + Alphabet
    (D) Ctrl key + Alphabet

13. Which keys will you use to type numbers quickly?
    (A) We will use the separate number keys at the right hand side of the key board.
    (B) We will press the Num lock and then use the separate number keypad at the right hand side.
    (C) We will use the horizontal number line on the top of the alphabets.
    (D) We will press Caps Lock and then use the separate number keypad at the right hand side.

14. What will happen when we use the following keys together?
    Shift + test
    (A) It will type: %^^&*
    (B) It will type TEST
    (C) It will type test
    (D) It will type 1234

15. Which key will you use to move to the last position in a row?
    (A) Insert
    (B) Home
    (C) Delete
    (D) End

16. Match the following correctly.

	Key	Output
(i)	Shift + R (caps lock off)	(a) B
(ii)	Caps Lock + b	(b) 12345
(iii)	Shift + 7	(c) R
(iv)	Num Lock + 12345	(d) &

(A) i-c, ii-a, iii-d, iv-b
(B) i-c, ii-b, iii-d, iv-a
(C) i-c, ii-d, iii-a, iv-b
(D) i-d, ii-a, iii-c, iv-b

17. Which set has all special keys in it?
    (A) Shift, alphabet, number
    (B) Shift, ctrl, number
    (C) Shift, F1, Tab
    (D) Alphabet, number, backspace

18. What is the pattern of the alphabet keys on the keyboard?
    (A) ABCD
    (B) QWTY
    (C) ASDFB
    (D) QWERTY

19. Match the following correctly.

Key		Function
(i)	Shift	(a) helps type capital alphabets
(ii)	—	(b) moves the cursor to the starting of the row
(iii)	|Home|	(c) special key helps in typing symbols
(iv)	Caps Lock	(d) navigates the cursor to left

(A) i-c, ii-b, iii-d, iv-a   (B) i-c, ii-a, iii-b, iv-d

(C) i-a, ii-d, iii-b, iv-c   (D) i-c, ii-d, iii-b, iv-a

20. What is wrong in the keyboard below?
(A) The number pad on the right is wrong.
(B) The alphabet key should be A, B, C, D in sequence.
(C) The symbol keys should be separate.
(D) The numbers should range from 1-10.

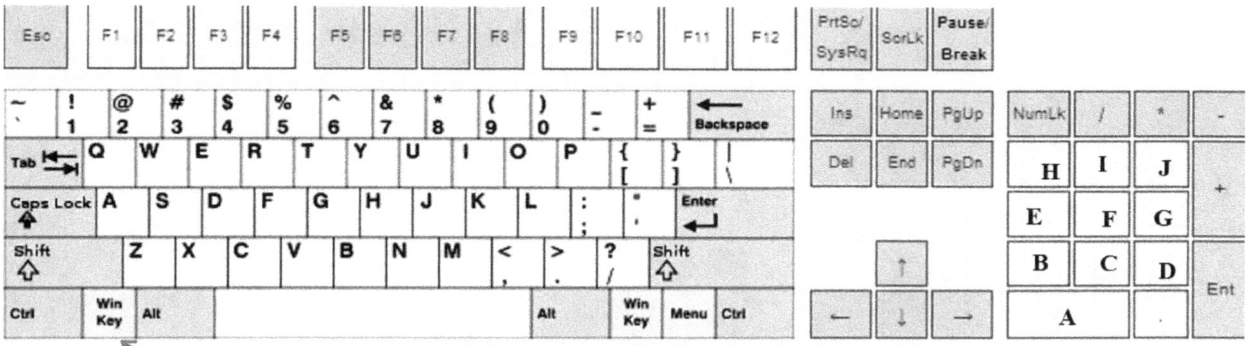

HOTS (ACHIEVERS SECTION)

21. The function of Caps Lock and Shift are same in case we want to
(A) Type a capital letter Y
(B) Type d
(C) Type @
(D) Type >

22. Which key will you use to close this function?

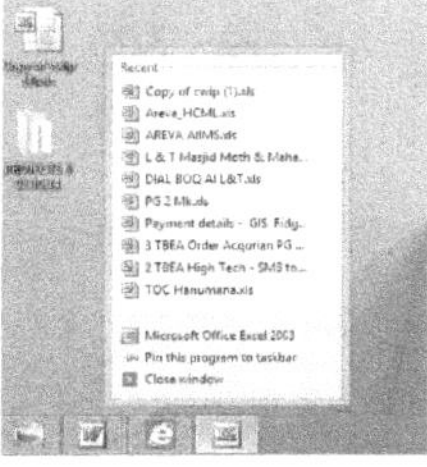

(A) F1

(B) Print Screen SysRq

(C) Backspace

(D) Esc

23. Small led light on the keyboard tells us capslock key is
(A) ON / OFF

(B) ON / ON

(C) OFF / OFF

24. Common between a keyboard, mobile, casio, calculator are.

(A) keys

(B) style

(C) size

25. The given device is of which type?

(A) Input

(B) Output

(C) Both input and output

(D) None of these

1.	Ⓐ Ⓑ Ⓒ Ⓓ	6.	Ⓐ Ⓑ Ⓒ Ⓓ	11.	Ⓐ Ⓑ Ⓒ Ⓓ	16.	Ⓐ Ⓑ Ⓒ Ⓓ	21.	Ⓐ Ⓑ Ⓒ Ⓓ
2.	Ⓐ Ⓑ Ⓒ Ⓓ	7.	Ⓐ Ⓑ Ⓒ Ⓓ	12.	Ⓐ Ⓑ Ⓒ Ⓓ	17.	Ⓐ Ⓑ Ⓒ Ⓓ	22.	Ⓐ Ⓑ Ⓒ Ⓓ
3.	Ⓐ Ⓑ Ⓒ Ⓓ	8.	Ⓐ Ⓑ Ⓒ Ⓓ	13.	Ⓐ Ⓑ Ⓒ Ⓓ	18.	Ⓐ Ⓑ Ⓒ Ⓓ	23.	Ⓐ Ⓑ Ⓒ Ⓓ
4.	Ⓐ Ⓑ Ⓒ Ⓓ	9.	Ⓐ Ⓑ Ⓒ Ⓓ	14.	Ⓐ Ⓑ Ⓒ Ⓓ	19.	Ⓐ Ⓑ Ⓒ Ⓓ	24.	Ⓐ Ⓑ Ⓒ Ⓓ
5.	Ⓐ Ⓑ Ⓒ Ⓓ	10.	Ⓐ Ⓑ Ⓒ Ⓓ	15.	Ⓐ Ⓑ Ⓒ Ⓓ	20.	Ⓐ Ⓑ Ⓒ Ⓓ	25.	Ⓐ Ⓑ Ⓒ Ⓓ

OLYMPIAD WORKBOOK (NCO) CLASS— 2

LEARNING TO USE MOUSE

LEARNING OBJECTIVES

➤ Mouse
➤ Types of Mouse
➤ Functioning of a Mouse

MULTIPLE CHOICE QUESTIONS

1. A mouse is a
   (A) Tracking device
   (B) An input device
   (C) An output device
   (D) A processing device

2. A mouse is connected with
   (A) A monitor
   (B) A CPU
   (C) A UPS
   (D) A switch board

3. Tick the wrong group.
   (A) Two-buttoned mouse, three-buttoned mouse
   (B) Three-buttoned mouse, scroll mouse
   (C) Scroll mouse, five button mouse
   (D) Laser mouse, Ball mouse

4. What is the slant arrow that represents the mouse on the monitor screen?
   (A) Mouse pointer (B) Cursor
   (C) Keyword   (D) Line

5. This moves when the mouse is moved manually.
   (A) Icon   (B) Files
   (C) Desktop (D) Cursor

6. This is not a mouse action.
   (A) Drag and drop
   (B) Refresh
   (C) Right click
   (D) Left click

7. This term is not related to a mouse.
   (A) Laser (B) Ball
   (C) Drag   (D) Keys

8. Mehul wants to open a picture on his desktop, what will he do?
   (A) He will double left click on the picture icon present on the desktop.
   (B) He will drag the picture present on the desktop.
   (C) He will right click on the picture and then drag it.
   (D) He will left click, once on the picture.

9. Match the following correctly.

Mouse action name		Function
(a) Right click	(i)	Moves an item from one place to another on the desktop

(b) Left single (ii) Opens the list of
    click   commands

(c) Left double (iii) Executes a function
    click   or opens a file or
                       program

(d) Drag and   (iv) Selects an item on
    Drop   the desktop

(A) a-iii, b-iv, c-ii, d-i

(B) a-ii, b-iv, c-iii, d-i

(C) a-iv, b-ii, c-iii, d-i

(D) a-ii, b-iv, c-i, d-iii

10. Observe the image below. What is happening in the image?

(A) The mouse has dragged the icon.
(B) The mouse has hover the icon.
(C) The mouse has opened the icon.
(D) The mouse has right clicked on the icon.

11. The central wheel of a mouse is known as __________.
(A) Trackball
(B) Rubber ball
(C) Scroll wheel
(D) Trackwheel

12. A ball mouse needs a __________ for support and movement.
(A) Mouse pad   (B) CPU
(C) Monitor   (D) UPS

13. Which part of the body do we use while using our mouse?
(A) Upper limbs
(B) Lower limbs
(C) Pelvic region
(D) Abdominal region

14. Some mouse devices have a light blinking on them. What is it?
(A) An electrical source
(B) A battery symbol
(C) A laser light
(D) A scroll wheel indicator

15. To complete an action of a mouse, we will
(A) Right click it
(B) We will double left click it
(C) We will drag and drop
(D) We will single left click

16. Which finger is used the most while using a mouse?
(A) Middle finger
(B) Index finger
(C) Thumb
(D) Smallest finger

17. This is not a pointing device.

(A) 
Trackball

(B) 
Mouse

(C) 
Stylus pen

(D) 
Speaker

18. Find the odd one out.

(A) 
Two buttoned
mouse

(B)
Scroll wheel
mouse

(C)
Joystick

(D)
Laser mouse

19. One of the following statements is false.
   (A) A mouse helps in playing games.
   (B) A mouse stores data.
   (C) A mouse helps in selecting a file.
   (D) A mouse may or may not have a connecting wire.

20. Mohit is organising icons on his desktop. Which mouse function will he use?
   (A) Drag and Drop
   (B) Right click
   (C) Left Click
   (D) Dragging the mouse

HOTS (ACHIEVERS SECTION)

21. Sachin wants to place the Recycle Bin icon at the topmost left corner of his desktop screen, How will he do this?

   (A) He will use double click action of the mouse.

   (B) He will use delete button of the keyboard.

   (C) He will use drag and drop function of the mouse.

   (D) He will right click on the icon.

22. I. Identify the following image.
    II. What will happen when you move your mouse cursor over it?

	I	II
(A)	Menu Bar	a menu will open
(B)	Taskbar	a small preview window is flashed
(C)	Menu Bar	a file will open
(D)	Taskbar	a list of items will be shown

23. What is happening in the image below?

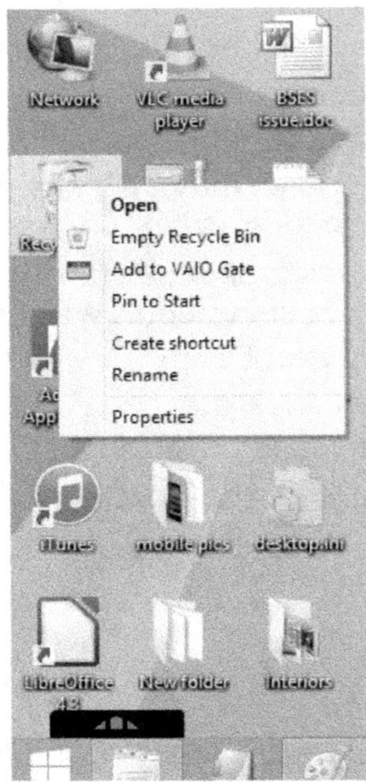

(A) The computer mouse has double clicked on the Recycle Bin icon.
(B) The computer mouse has right clicked on the Recycle Bin icon.
(C) The computer mouse has left clicked on the Recycle Bin icon.
(D) The computer mouse has dragged the Recycle Bin icon.

24. The word 'Mouse' is very much popular in computer world. The word 'Mouse' is originated at the
(A) Stanford Research Institute
(B) American Research Institute
(C) Spanish Research Institute
(D) Cambridge Research

25. The _______ of the mouse pointer changes according to the task and application.
(A) style   (B) colour
(C) shape   (D) size

—————Darken Your Choice with HB Pencil—————

1.	Ⓐ Ⓑ Ⓒ Ⓓ	6.	Ⓐ Ⓑ Ⓒ Ⓓ	11.	Ⓐ Ⓑ Ⓒ Ⓓ	16.	Ⓐ Ⓑ Ⓒ Ⓓ	21.	Ⓐ Ⓑ Ⓒ Ⓓ
2.	Ⓐ Ⓑ Ⓒ Ⓓ	7.	Ⓐ Ⓑ Ⓒ Ⓓ	12.	Ⓐ Ⓑ Ⓒ Ⓓ	17.	Ⓐ Ⓑ Ⓒ Ⓓ	22.	Ⓐ Ⓑ Ⓒ Ⓓ
3.	Ⓐ Ⓑ Ⓒ Ⓓ	8.	Ⓐ Ⓑ Ⓒ Ⓓ	13.	Ⓐ Ⓑ Ⓒ Ⓓ	18.	Ⓐ Ⓑ Ⓒ Ⓓ	23.	Ⓐ Ⓑ Ⓒ Ⓓ
4.	Ⓐ Ⓑ Ⓒ Ⓓ	9.	Ⓐ Ⓑ Ⓒ Ⓓ	14.	Ⓐ Ⓑ Ⓒ Ⓓ	19.	Ⓐ Ⓑ Ⓒ Ⓓ	24.	Ⓐ Ⓑ Ⓒ Ⓓ
5.	Ⓐ Ⓑ Ⓒ Ⓓ	10.	Ⓐ Ⓑ Ⓒ Ⓓ	15.	Ⓐ Ⓑ Ⓒ Ⓓ	20.	Ⓐ Ⓑ Ⓒ Ⓓ	25.	Ⓐ Ⓑ Ⓒ Ⓓ

INTRODUCTION TO MS PAINT

LEARNING OBJECTIVES

➤ MS Paint – A Colourful Software
➤ Opening MS Paint
➤ Components of a Paint Window

MULTIPLE CHOICE QUESTIONS

1. What is MS Paint?
   (A) A writing tool
   (B) A drawing tool
   (C) A gaming tool
   (D) A music tool

2. When you open a new paint file, what appears on the title bar?
   (A) Untitled-Paint
   (B) 1-Paint
   (C) New-Paint
   (D) First-Paint

3. Where is quick access toolbar located?
   (A) It is located above the title bar.
   (B) It is located vertically on the left side
   (C) It is located on the left side of the title bar.
   (D) It is located in the ribbon.

4. Which tool helps us draw free-form drawing?
   (A) ✏
   (B) **A**
   (C) ╲
   (D) 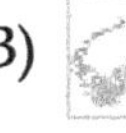
   Brushes

5. Which tool is part of the shapes window?
   (A) 🔍   (B) **A**
   (C) 'O| (D) ◊

6. Which colour button will you use for foreground colour?
   (A) Color 1   (B) Color 2
   (C) Edit colors   (D) Brushes

7. We cannot fill colour in a
   (A) Circle   (B) Rectangle
   (C) Star   (D) Curved line

8. We can have a colour spray effect with this tool.
   (A)   (B)
   (C)   (D)

9. Observe the image below and tick the correct set of tools used to get this image.

   (A) Line tool
   (B) Line and brush tool
   (C) Line tool and size tool
   (D) Line tool and pencil tool

10. What is the difference between I and II?

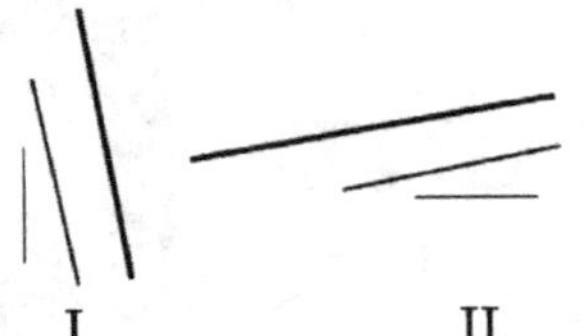

I   II

(A) Image I is made by line tool and image II by pencil.
(B) Image I is rotated to 90° to get image II.
(C) Image I and II has no difference.
(D) Image I has longer lines than image II.

11. Both the following tools belong to

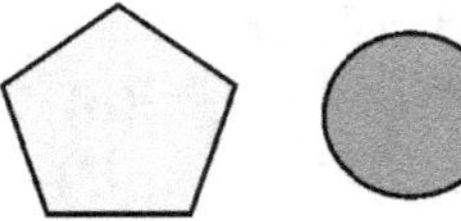

(A) Shapes tab
(B) Colors tab
(C) Brushes tab
(D) Selection button

12. The following image could be produced using spray can?

(A) Shape tool, brush tool, line tool and colour
(B) Shapes, colour and colour fill
(C) Shape tool, line tool and colour
(D) Shape tool, colour fill, line tool and colour

13. Which is the best suited answer for the following question? Define select tool.
(A) Selects a part of a picture
(B) Selects the complete picture
(C) Selects a rectangular or free form part of the picture
(D) Can select, rectangular or free form shape of the picture or the entire picture.

14. Mohit has created an image of a flower, but when he took its printout, the image was very small in size. Which tool will he use to increase the image size?
(A) Select and rotate
(B) Select and resize
(C) Select and crop
(D) Resize

15. Look at the images shown below. Which is labelled incorrectly?

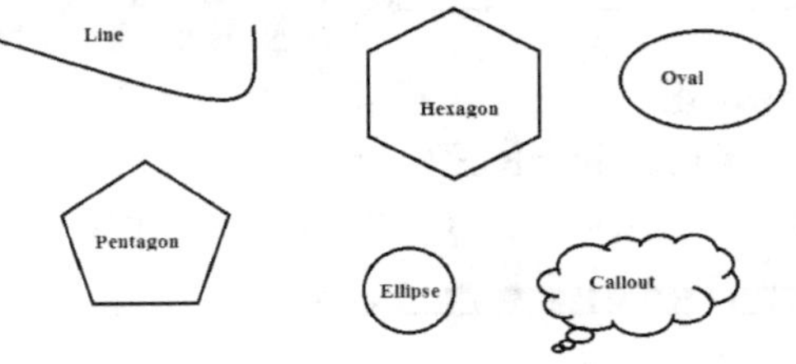

(A) Line, ellipse and call out
(B) Line and ellipse
(C) Ellipse
(D) Call out and ellipse

16. What is this area?

(A) Quick access toolbar
(B) Ribbon
(C) Clipboard in Ribbon
(D) Editing tools

17. Match the following correctly.

Tool		Function
(a)		(i) Polygon shape
(b)		(ii) Flip the picture or selection
(c)	Rotate	(iii) Erase part of the picture
(d)		(iv) Star shape

OLYMPIAD WORKBOOK (NCO) CLASS – 2

(A) a-ii, b-iii, c-iv, d-i

(B) a-iii, b-ii, c-iv, d-i

(C) a-ii, b-iii, c-i, d-iv

(D) a-iii, b-iv, c-ii, d-i

18. Under which head can we open a new paint file?

(A) Home tab

(B) Quick access toolbar

(C) Quick access toolbar or File Menu

(D) File menu

19. Amita wants to create the following image, how will she do it?

(A) She will use shapes.

(B) She will use shapes, cut and copy button.

(C) She will use shapes and copy, and paste repeatedly.

(D) She will use shapes and copy.

20. How many styles of brushes are there?

(A) 8   (B) 10

(C) 6   (D) 9

HOTS (ACHIEVERS SECTION)

21. Which image is the most clear and why?

 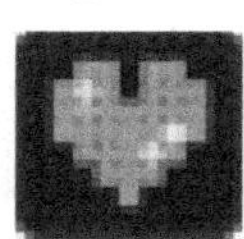  

I   II   III   IV

(A) IV, because we can count the dots properly

(B) III and IV as we can identify the colours properly

(C) IV as it has the highest pixels

(D) IV because of the colour contrast

22. Michael pasted her son's picture on a paint file.

Describe what did she do?

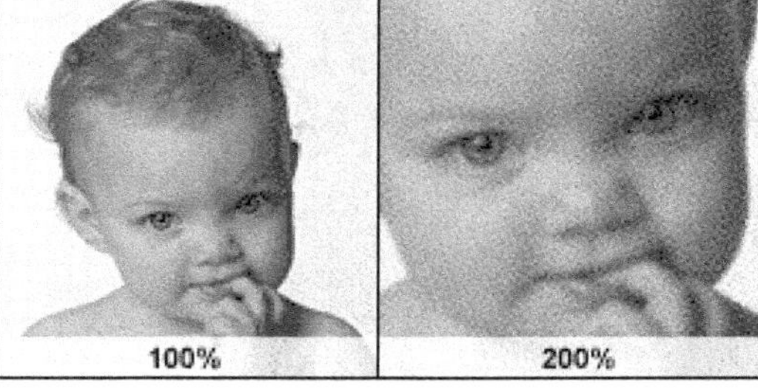

(A) She pasted two images.

(B) She pasted an image and then zoomed it.

(C) She copied the first image and then zoomed it.

(D) She pasted two different images.

Look at the following MS Paint window and answer questions 3–5.

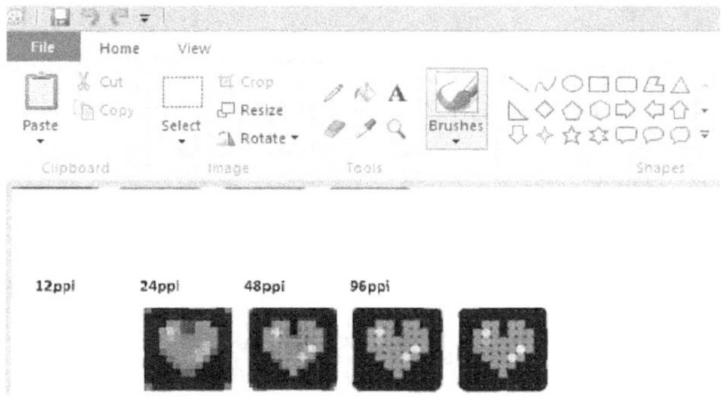

23. If you want to remove the numbers in the picture. What will you use?

(A)    (B)

(C) [ ] Select   (D)

24. If you want to close the MS Paint window, which button will you use?

(A) ×

(B) 💾 ↺ ↻ ≡ |

(C) 💾 ↺ ↻ ≡ | and ×

(D) Home   View

25. In the above MS Paint window, you are supposed to enclose the image into an enclosure and fill it with various colours. How many tools will you use?

(A) [colour palette] and [fill]

(B)  Shapes , Color 1 Color 2 and [fill]

(C) Brushes

(D) [colour palette] and Brushes

🕐🕐🕐

LATEST DEVELOPMENTS IN IT

8

➤ Latest developments in the field of IT

MULTIPLE CHOICE QUESTIONS

1. Identify the icon: It is a/an ….

   (A) iOS   (B) OS
   (C) Game   (D) Social App

2. Mobile app is a kind of
   (A) Game
   (B) Social network
   (C) Software
   (D) Mailing app

3. This is not a mobile app
   (A) iOS   (B) MS Paint
   (C) Temple Run   (D) Instagram

4. IT is used in
   (A) Medical sector
   (B) Army sector
   (C) Education sector
   (D) All the above

5. The following card involves computers for its operation
   (A) A Birthday Card
   (B) A Christmas Card
   (C) A Visiting Card
   (D) A Credit Card

6. The following icon belongs to

   (A) Lumia   (B) Samsung
   (C) Apple   (D) Blackberry

Directions (7-10): Identify the following images.

7. 

   (A) Smileys   (B) App
   (C) Game   (D) OS

8. 

   (A) Software   (B) OS
   (C) Gaming software   (D) iOS

9. 

(A) Social networking site with an e-Book reader advertisement
(B) e-Book reader advertisement
(C) Social networking site
(D) Android app

10. 

(A) Flying robot
(B) Flying camera
(C) Toy helicopter
(D) Remote controlled toy

11. Through this we connect to the internet
(A) 3G
(B) Telephone
(C) WiFi and 3G
(D) Television

12. This is the smallest smart device.
(A) iPad
(B) iPhone
(C) Tablet
(D) Laptop

13. 

Who will help the umpire take the decision?
(A) The bowler
(B) The audience
(C) A Drone
(D) A computer

14. Which is the best suited definition for a smartphone?
(A) A big-screen phone
(B) A mobile phone that performs many of the functions of a computer
(C) A phone with touchscreen
(D) A phone with lots of games

15. 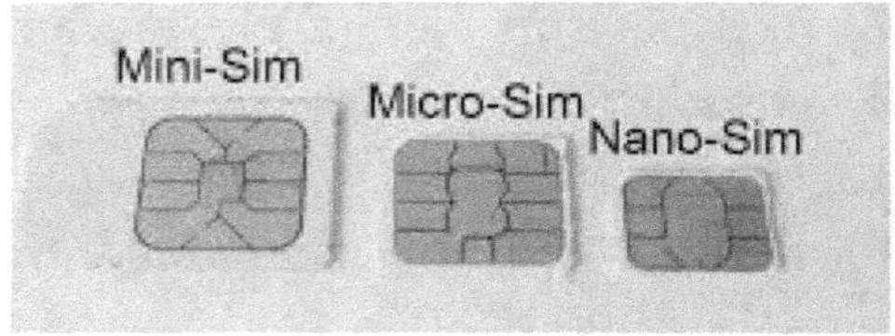

What are the children wearing?
(A) A magical gadget
(B) A 3-D glass
(C) A sun glass
(D) A toy

16. Android is developed by
(A) Microsoft
(B) Adobe
(C) Mozilla
(D) Google

17. Which OS has its versions named based on various sugary products?
(A) Android
(B) Windows
(C) Adobe
(D) Mac

18. Which is the latest version of Android?
(A) KitKat
(B) Lollipop
(C) Gingerbread
(D) None of these

19. This is an anti-virus program.
(A) McAfee
(B) MS Paint
(C) Hill Climber
(D) Candy Crush

20. Where can you insert this kind of object?

(A) Computer
(B) Mobile
(C) Mobile and computer
(D) Mobile and tablet

21. The following device is specialised for

(A) Reading books
(B) It is an electronic library for reading books.
(C) It is a document creator.
(D) It is an iPad.

22. Which device is the latest invention?

(A) 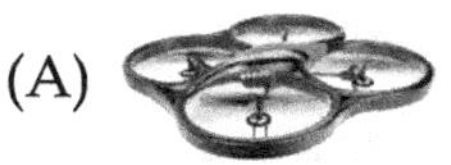   (B) 

(C)    (D) 

23. The given device can be read by __________.

(A) Smartphones
(B) Tablets
(C) Calculators
(D) Both (A) and (B)

24. This is an image of which operating system version on Android?

(A) Lollipop   (B) Jellybean
(C) Kitkat   (D) Cupcake

25. This is an image of which operating system version on Android?

(A) Donut   (B) Lollipop
(C) Cupcake   (D) Honeycomb

―Darken Your Choice with HB Pencil―

1.	Ⓐ Ⓑ Ⓒ Ⓓ	6.	Ⓐ Ⓑ Ⓒ Ⓓ	11.	Ⓐ Ⓑ Ⓒ Ⓓ	16.	Ⓐ Ⓑ Ⓒ Ⓓ	21.	Ⓐ Ⓑ Ⓒ Ⓓ
2.	Ⓐ Ⓑ Ⓒ Ⓓ	7.	Ⓐ Ⓑ Ⓒ Ⓓ	12.	Ⓐ Ⓑ Ⓒ Ⓓ	17.	Ⓐ Ⓑ Ⓒ Ⓓ	22.	Ⓐ Ⓑ Ⓒ Ⓓ
3.	Ⓐ Ⓑ Ⓒ Ⓓ	8.	Ⓐ Ⓑ Ⓒ Ⓓ	13.	Ⓐ Ⓑ Ⓒ Ⓓ	18.	Ⓐ Ⓑ Ⓒ Ⓓ	23.	Ⓐ Ⓑ Ⓒ Ⓓ
4.	Ⓐ Ⓑ Ⓒ Ⓓ	9.	Ⓐ Ⓑ Ⓒ Ⓓ	14.	Ⓐ Ⓑ Ⓒ Ⓓ	19.	Ⓐ Ⓑ Ⓒ Ⓓ	24.	Ⓐ Ⓑ Ⓒ Ⓓ
5.	Ⓐ Ⓑ Ⓒ Ⓓ	10.	Ⓐ Ⓑ Ⓒ Ⓓ	15.	Ⓐ Ⓑ Ⓒ Ⓓ	20.	Ⓐ Ⓑ Ⓒ Ⓓ	25.	Ⓐ Ⓑ Ⓒ Ⓓ

LOGICAL REASONING

LEARNING OBJECTIVES

➤ Finding the missing part in a figure
➤ Odd One Out
➤ Number Series
➤ Ranking Test
➤ Identification of the main figure
➤ Grouping of Figures

MULTIPLE CHOICE QUESTIONS

1. Find the missing number in the given number pattern, if the series in both the patterns follows the same rule.

Pattern-I	Pattern-II
22	60
30	68
38	?

(A) 76   (B) 66
(C) 36   (D) 56

2. Find the missing number in the given number pattern.
80, 70, 55, 45, ?
(A) 25   (B) 30
(C) 20   (D) 35

3. Complete the pattern by choosing the next figure.

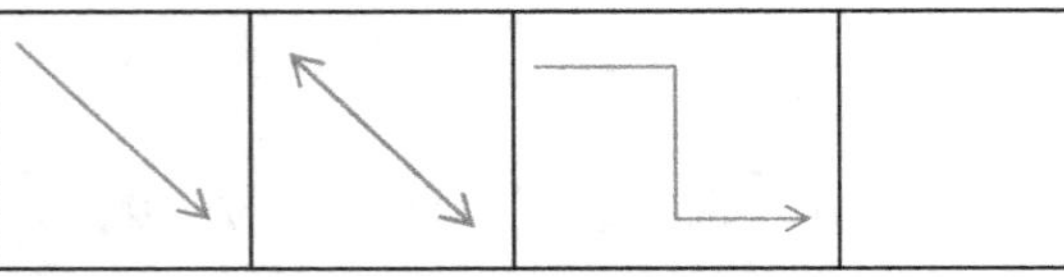

(A)   (B)

(C)   (D)

4. Choose the odd one out.

(A)   (B)

(C)   (D)

5. Choose the odd one out.
16, 20, 24, 28, 32, 38, 40
(A) 20   (B) 28
(C) 33   (D) 38

6. Choose the odd one out.

(A)   (B)

(C)   (D)

7. Find the next number in the series.
40, 30, 22, 16, ?
(A) 14   (B) 12
(C) 10   (D) 18

8. Find the next number in the series.
1, 3, 9, 27, 81, ?
(A) 243   (B) 253
(C) 250   (D) 216

9. Find the next number in the series.
2, 4, 12, 24, 72, 144, ?

(A) 288   (B) 382
(C) 432   (D) 576

10. Find out the relation.

    Pen : Ink : : Pencil : ?
    (A) Iron   (B) Plastic
    (C) Graphite   (D) Carbon

11. Find out the relation.

    Uttarakhand: Dehradun : : Goa: ?
    (A) Patna
    (B) Panaji
    (C) Jaipur
    (D) Gandhinagar

12. Find the missing shape by identifying the relationship.

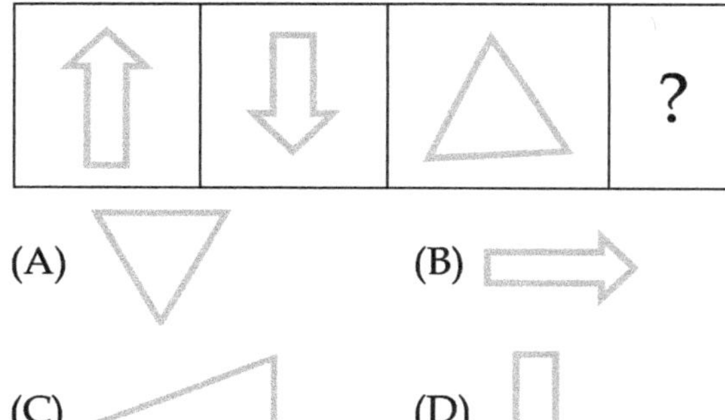

(A)   (B)

(C)   (D)

Directions (13–15):

Alphabet in natural series are:

A = 1	B = 2	C = 3	D = 4	E = 5	F = 6
G = 7	H = 8	I = 9	J = 10	K = 11	L = 12
M = 13	N = 14	O = 15	P = 16	Q = 17	R = 18
S = 19	T = 20	U = 21	V = 22	W = 23	X = 24
Y = 25	Z = 26				

13. If TABLE is written as 40, then CHAIR will be written as ______.
    (A) 39
    (B) 38
    (C) 26
    (D) 36

14. If CARROT = 75, then RADISH will be written as ______.

(A) 76
(B) 36
(C) 59
(D) 85

15. If SEA = 13, then YAK will be written as ______.
    (A) 16
    (B) 13
    (C) 17
    (D) 8

Direction (16-18): Observe the given figure carefully and answer the following questions.

Left (first)

16. Which bird is seventh from the right end?
    (A) M   (B) L
    (C) N   (D) P

17. Bird O is second to the right of bird ______.
    (A) P   (B) I
    (C) M   (D) N

18. If bird P and I interchange their positions, then bird ______ is at the left end.
    (A) I   (B) L
    (C) P   (D) M

Directions (19–23): Which of the following figures is hidden or embedded in the given figure?

19.

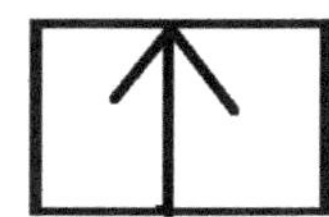

(A)

(B) 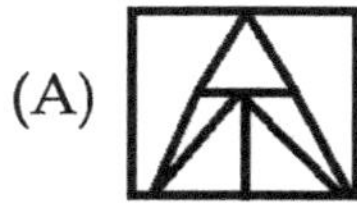

(C) 

(D) 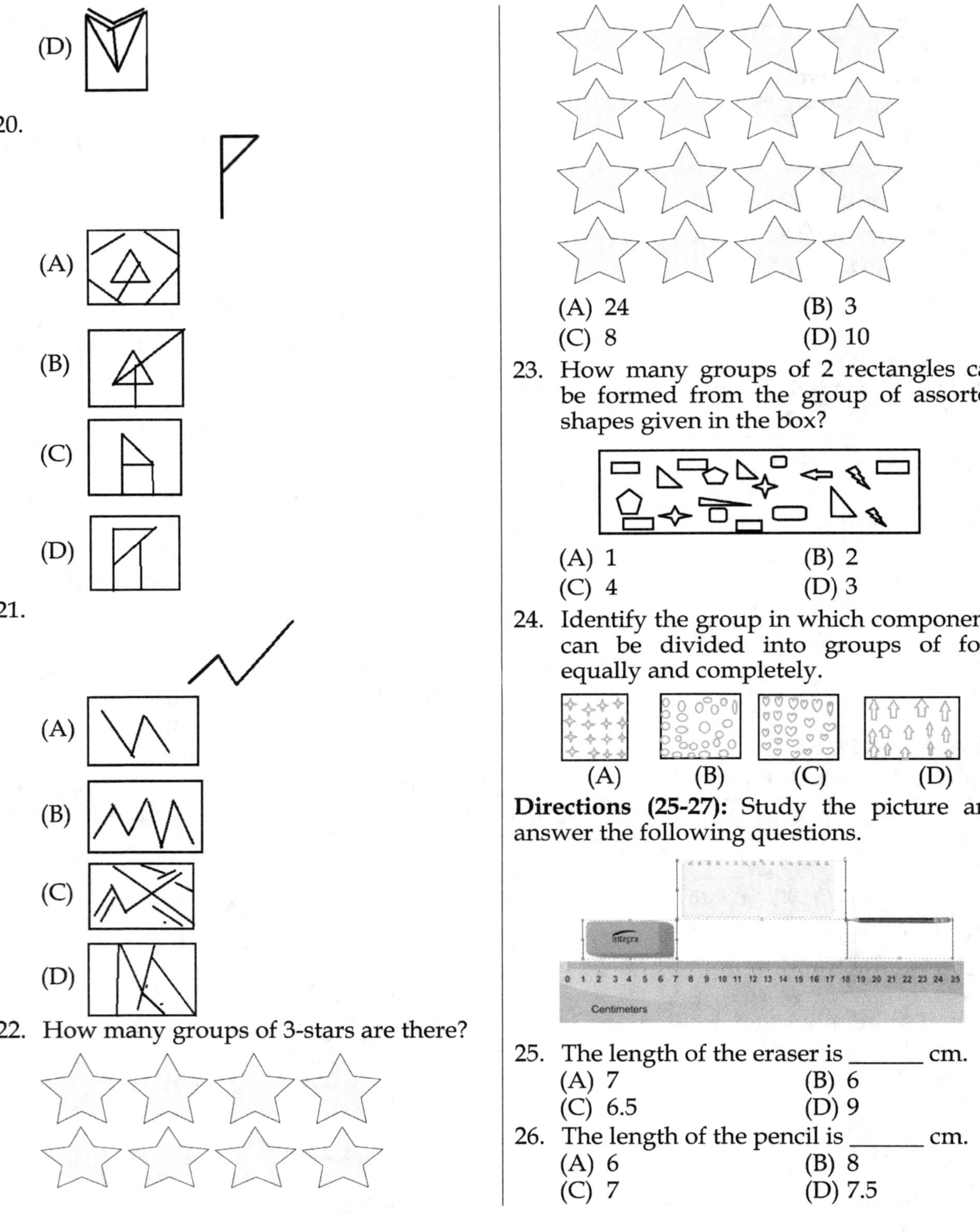

20.

(A)

(B)

(C)

(D)

21.

(A)

(B)

(C)

(D)

22. How many groups of 3-stars are there?

(A) 24   (B) 3
(C) 8   (D) 10

23. How many groups of 2 rectangles can be formed from the group of assorted shapes given in the box?

(A) 1   (B) 2
(C) 4   (D) 3

24. Identify the group in which components can be divided into groups of four equally and completely.

(A)   (B)   (C)   (D)

Directions (25-27): Study the picture and answer the following questions.

25. The length of the eraser is _______ cm.
(A) 7   (B) 6
(C) 6.5   (D) 9

26. The length of the pencil is _______ cm.
(A) 6   (B) 8
(C) 7   (D) 7.5

OLYMPIAD WORKBOOK (NCO) CLASS– 2

27. Eraser is ____ cm shorter than the pencil.
   (A) 1 cm   (B) 3 cm
   (C) 2 cm   (D) 0.5 cm

28. The figure given below is made up of ______ triangles.

   (A) 5   (B) 6
   (C) 7   (D) 8

29. Which two shapes form the given figure?

   (A) Rhombus and square
   (B) Triangle and square
   (C) Kite and rhombus
   (D) Rectangle and triangle

30. Which two types of geometrical shapes are hidden in the given picture?

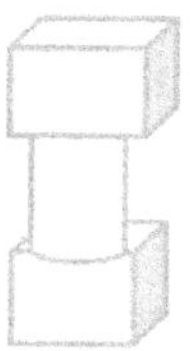

   (A) Square and cylinder
   (B) Rectangle and cylinder
   (C) Cubes and cylinder
   (D) Rectangle and cubes

1.	Ⓐ Ⓑ Ⓒ Ⓓ	7.	Ⓐ Ⓑ Ⓒ Ⓓ	13.	Ⓐ Ⓑ Ⓒ Ⓓ	19.	Ⓐ Ⓑ Ⓒ Ⓓ	25.	Ⓐ Ⓑ Ⓒ Ⓓ
2.	Ⓐ Ⓑ Ⓒ Ⓓ	8.	Ⓐ Ⓑ Ⓒ Ⓓ	14.	Ⓐ Ⓑ Ⓒ Ⓓ	20.	Ⓐ Ⓑ Ⓒ Ⓓ	26.	Ⓐ Ⓑ Ⓒ Ⓓ
3.	Ⓐ Ⓑ Ⓒ Ⓓ	9.	Ⓐ Ⓑ Ⓒ Ⓓ	15.	Ⓐ Ⓑ Ⓒ Ⓓ	21.	Ⓐ Ⓑ Ⓒ Ⓓ	27.	Ⓐ Ⓑ Ⓒ Ⓓ
4.	Ⓐ Ⓑ Ⓒ Ⓓ	10.	Ⓐ Ⓑ Ⓒ Ⓓ	16.	Ⓐ Ⓑ Ⓒ Ⓓ	22.	Ⓐ Ⓑ Ⓒ Ⓓ	28.	Ⓐ Ⓑ Ⓒ Ⓓ
5.	Ⓐ Ⓑ Ⓒ Ⓓ	11.	Ⓐ Ⓑ Ⓒ Ⓓ	17.	Ⓐ Ⓑ Ⓒ Ⓓ	23.	Ⓐ Ⓑ Ⓒ Ⓓ	29.	Ⓐ Ⓑ Ⓒ Ⓓ
6.	Ⓐ Ⓑ Ⓒ Ⓓ	12.	Ⓐ Ⓑ Ⓒ Ⓓ	18.	Ⓐ Ⓑ Ⓒ Ⓓ	24.	Ⓐ Ⓑ Ⓒ Ⓓ	30.	Ⓐ Ⓑ Ⓒ Ⓓ

MODEL TEST PAPER

1. Find the missing number.

Pattern-I	Pattern-II
52	29
64	41
76	?

   (A) 40   (B) 53

   (C) 51   (D) 56

2. Who am I?

   (a) My hundred's digit is 8.

   (b) My ten's digit is 5.

   (c) My one's digit is 4 more than my ten's digit.

   (A) 859   (B) 858

   (C) 856   (D) 857

3. Swati is taller than Ananya. Ananya is taller than Aishwarya. Aishwarya is taller than Priya. Who is the shortest girl?

   (A) Swati   (B) Ananya

   (C) Aishwarya   (D) Priya

4. If yesterday was Thursday, then tomorrow will be ______.

   (A) Friday   (B) Thursday

   (C) Saturday   (D) Sunday

5. ______ is needed to buy the toy car shown below.

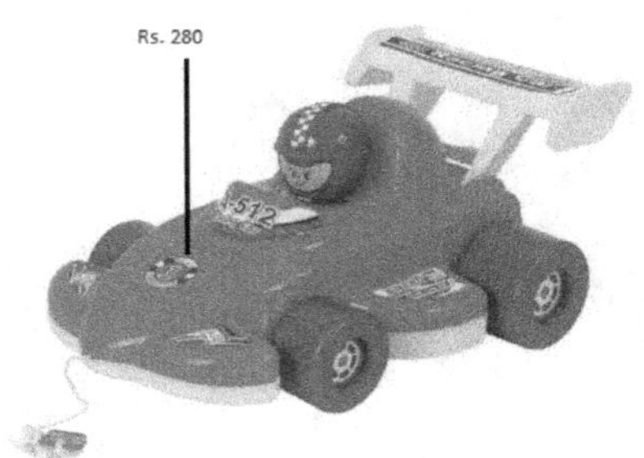

   (A) One 100-rupee, one 50-rupee, and two 10-rupee

   (B) Two 100-rupee, one 50-rupee, and three 10-rupee

   (C) One 100-rupee, one 50-rupee, and three 10-rupee

   (D) Two 100-rupee, two 50-rupee, and two 10-rupee

6. How many more triangles are there in the box than rectangles?

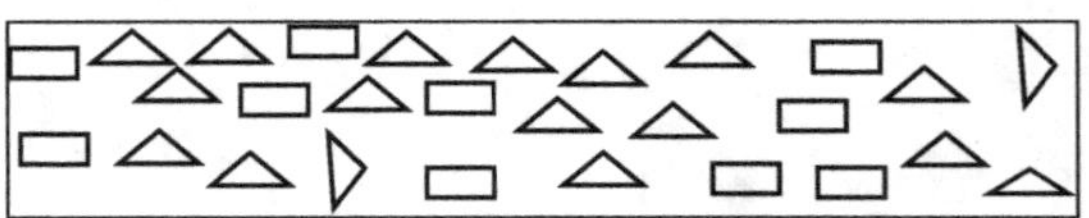

   (A) 8   (B) 10

   (C) 11   (D) 7

7. Amit resides on the second floor of the building. There are total 22 stairs to reach his house. How many stairs are there between 8th and 22nd steps?

   (A) 12   (B) 13

   (C) 16   (D 18

8. If Sumit and Shourya interchange their positions, who will be the nearest to the house?

  1. Kunal   2. Sumit   3. Shourya   4. Raj

(A) Kunal   (B) Sumit
(C) Shourya   (D) Raj

9. What will be the number of balls in each row, when three equal groups of 18 balls are made?

(A) 4   (B) 5
(C) 6   (D) 7

10. Which flower is the fifth to the left of the flower M?

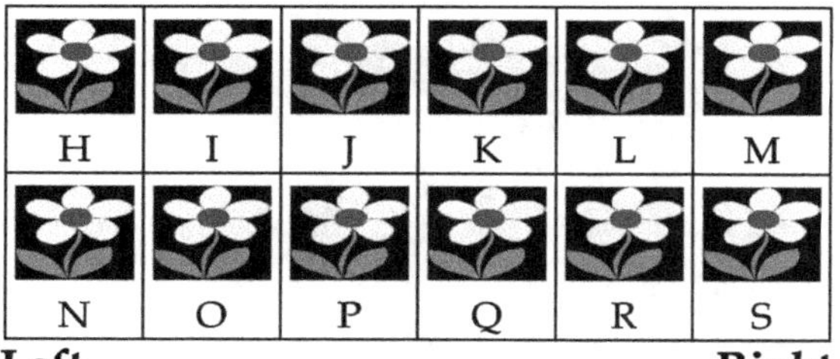

| H | I | J | K | L | M |
| N | O | P | Q | R | S |

Left   **Right**

(A) S   (B) R
(C) I   (D) H

11. Which of the following figures give incorrect number relation?

12. Which of the following item is the shortest?

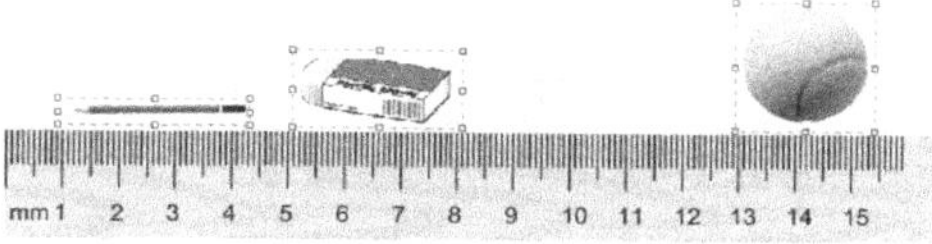

(A) Ball   (B) Pencil
(C) Sharpener   (D) Blade

13. Find the number of people in the queue, if I am second from the right, but fifth from the left.

(A) 6   (B) 7
(C) 8   (D) 9

14. What is to the South of the House?

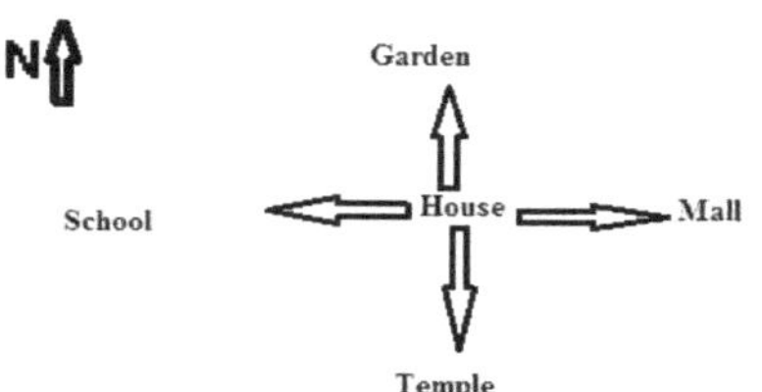

(A) Mall   (B) Garden
(C) School   (D) Temple

15. Swayam watched a cartoon programme which lasted 40 minutes. The programme ended at 3.30 p.m. The programme started at ______.

(A) 2.50 pm   (B) 2.40 pm
(C) 3.00 pm   (D) 2.55 pm

Computers

16. Match column I and column II and choose the correct option.

	Column-I		Column-II
(a)	Connecting wires	(i)	Used for huge mathematical calculations
(b)	Abacus	(ii)	Connect different parts of computers
(c)	Arithmetic and logic unit	(iii)	Part of CPU
(d)	Mainframe computers	(iv)	First calculating device used by man

(A) a-ii, b-iv, c-iii, d-i
(B) a-i, b-ii, c-iii, d-iv
(C) a-iv, b-i, c-iii, d-ii
(D) a-iv, b-ii, c-iii, d-i

17. This process occurs when the computer is already ON and you restart it using the Restart option in the Start Menu.
(A) Warm boot
(B) Cool boot
(C) Freeze boot
(D) Running boot

18. These are the only two binary digits of a binary system that can be read by a computer.
(A) 9 & 10 (B) 0 & 10
(C) 0 & 1 (D) 1 & 2

19. Who am I?
(i) I am an electronic device.
(ii) I help to run the computer even during power failure.

(A) (B) 
(C) (D)

20. This part of a computer is called the brain of the computer.
(A) Keyboard (B) Monitor
(C) Disks (D) CPU

21. Match column I and column II and choose the correct option.
(a) Computer in office (i) Passbook
(b) Computer in school (ii) Textbooks
(c) Computer in banks (iii) Record books
(d) Computer in railways (iv) Tickets

(A) a-ii, b-iii, c-i, d-iv
(B) a-iii, b-ii, c-iv, d-i
(C) a-iv, b-ii, c-i, d-iii
(D) a-iii, b-ii, c-i, d-iv

22. Look at the picture given below and answer the following question:

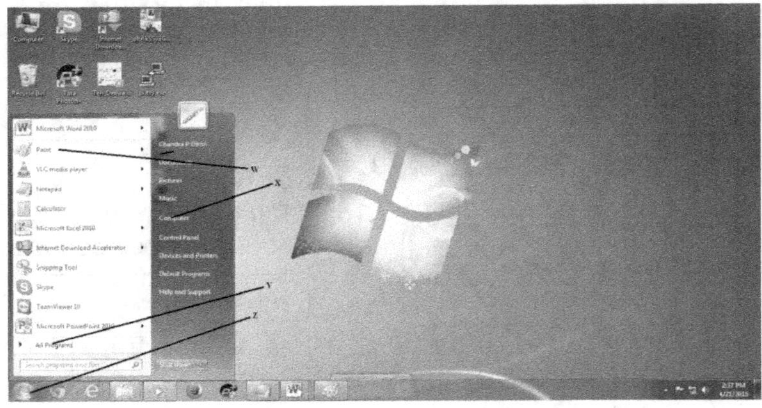

Sonu wants to draw an image. Which button will she click with her mouse?
(A) X (B) W (C) Y (D) Z

23. Select the correct key combination to get the @ symbol.
(A) Shift + 1
(B) Shift + 2
(C) Shift + 3
(D) Shift + 4

24. Look at the following pictures and match the correct key with the application.

List-1

(A) When we type something wrong
(B) To write Sanchit's name

(C) To write roll numbers of my classmates

(D) To go back to the previous page

List-2

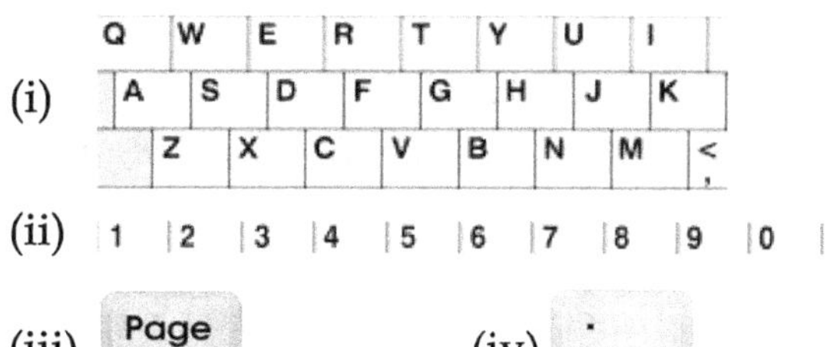

(i)

(ii)

(iii)

(iv)

(A) a-ii, b-iv, c-i, d-iii

(B) a-iii, b-iv, c-I, d-ii

(C) a-iv, b-i, c-ii, d-iii

(D) a-i, b-iv, c-ii, d-iii

25. This term is not related to the computer mouse.

(A) Left click   (B) Right click

(C) Middle click   (D) Double click

26. Match column I and column II and select the correct option.

	Column-I		Column-II
(a)	Selects an item	(i)	Double click
(b)	Opens a window	(ii)	Right click
(c)	Moves an item on the monitor	(iii)	Single click
(d)	Shows the list of commands	(iv)	Drag and Drop

(A) a-i, b-ii, c-iii, d-iv

(B) a-iii, b-i, c-iv, d-ii

(C) a-iv, b-i, c-ii, d-iii

(D) a-ii, b-i, c-iv, d-iii

Direction (27–28): Look at the picture given below and answer the questions based on the picture.

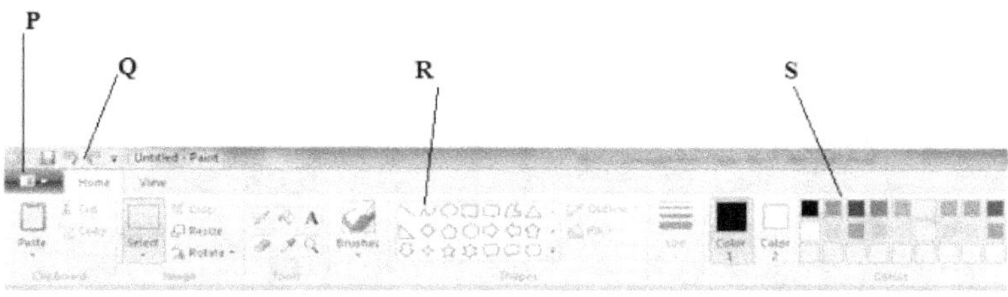

27. This area is called the Quick Access Toolbar.

(A) P   (B) Q

(C) R   (D) S

28. I help in drawing different shapes in MS Paint. I am also called the shape box. I am marked as ______ in the above figure.

(A) P   (B) Q

(C) R   (D) S

29. Mr. Bean brought a new phone recently. It has a nice big-screen. It has Android Operating System. Which of the following is the latest version of Android Operating System?

(A) Jelly Bean   (B) Gingerbread

(C) Lollipop   (D) Ice Cream

30. Small pictures present on the monitor screen are

(A) Taskbar   (B) Start button

(C) Files   (D) Icons

Achievers Section

31. Select the correct option.

(I) What is Vita?

(II) What is Wii?

	Column-I	Column–II
(a)	Vita is a version of a popular series of TV show	The name of a popular computer operating system
(b)	Vita is a version of a popular gaming device	Wii is a small handheld video game device produced by Nintendo.

(c)	Vita is a version of a popular TV device	A latest mobile phone
(d)	Vita is a version of a popular Computer device	A wireless internet device

32. Match Column I and Column II:

	I		**II**
(a)	The working speed of computer is	(i)	joystick
(b)	Computer is an	(ii)	Input device
(c)	It is used to show results.	(iii)	fast
(d)	It is used to play games.	(iv)	Electronic device

(A) a-ii, b-iii, c-iv, d-i

(B) a-iv, b-ii, c-i, d-iii

(C) a-iii, b-iv, c-ii, d-i

(D) a-ii, b-iv, c-i, d-iii

33. The data that is stored in a computer is known as

(A) Software   (B) Output

(C) Information   (D) Soft copy

34. The following information about a CPU is true.

(A) It is a miniprocessor of 1 inch square dimension and is made up of silicon.

(B) It is a microprocessor of 1 inch square dimension and is made up of silicon.

(C) It is a microprocessor of 1 inch square dimension and is made up of wires.

(D) It is a microprocessor of 2 inch square dimension and is made up of silicon.

35. Observe the image below and label the two components:

	I		**II**
(A)	Taskbar	(i)	System tray
(B)	System tray	(ii)	Taskbar
(C)	Icon	(iii)	System tray
(D)	Taskbar	(iv)	Clock

Darken Your Choice with HB Pencil

1.	Ⓐ Ⓑ Ⓒ Ⓓ	8.	Ⓐ Ⓑ Ⓒ Ⓓ	15.	Ⓐ Ⓑ Ⓒ Ⓓ	22.	Ⓐ Ⓑ Ⓒ Ⓓ	29.	Ⓐ Ⓑ Ⓒ Ⓓ
2.	Ⓐ Ⓑ Ⓒ Ⓓ	9.	Ⓐ Ⓑ Ⓒ Ⓓ	16.	Ⓐ Ⓑ Ⓒ Ⓓ	23.	Ⓐ Ⓑ Ⓒ Ⓓ	30.	Ⓐ Ⓑ Ⓒ Ⓓ
3.	Ⓐ Ⓑ Ⓒ Ⓓ	10.	Ⓐ Ⓑ Ⓒ Ⓓ	17.	Ⓐ Ⓑ Ⓒ Ⓓ	24.	Ⓐ Ⓑ Ⓒ Ⓓ	31.	Ⓐ Ⓑ Ⓒ Ⓓ
4.	Ⓐ Ⓑ Ⓒ Ⓓ	11.	Ⓐ Ⓑ Ⓒ Ⓓ	18.	Ⓐ Ⓑ Ⓒ Ⓓ	25.	Ⓐ Ⓑ Ⓒ Ⓓ	32.	Ⓐ Ⓑ Ⓒ Ⓓ
5.	Ⓐ Ⓑ Ⓒ Ⓓ	12.	Ⓐ Ⓑ Ⓒ Ⓓ	19.	Ⓐ Ⓑ Ⓒ Ⓓ	26.	Ⓐ Ⓑ Ⓒ Ⓓ	33.	Ⓐ Ⓑ Ⓒ Ⓓ
6.	Ⓐ Ⓑ Ⓒ Ⓓ	13.	Ⓐ Ⓑ Ⓒ Ⓓ	20.	Ⓐ Ⓑ Ⓒ Ⓓ	27.	Ⓐ Ⓑ Ⓒ Ⓓ	34.	Ⓐ Ⓑ Ⓒ Ⓓ
7.	Ⓐ Ⓑ Ⓒ Ⓓ	14.	Ⓐ Ⓑ Ⓒ Ⓓ	21.	Ⓐ Ⓑ Ⓒ Ⓓ	28.	Ⓐ Ⓑ Ⓒ Ⓓ	35.	Ⓐ Ⓑ Ⓒ Ⓓ

OLYMPIAD WORKBOOK (NCO) CLASS – 2

HINTS AND SOLUTIONS

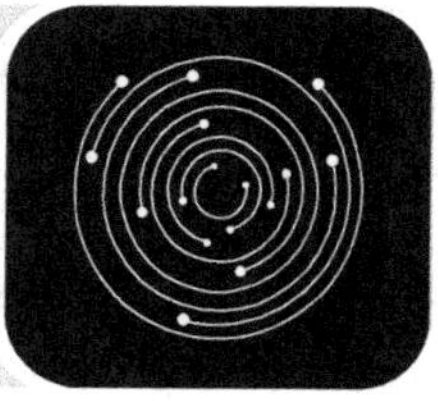

1. INTRODUCTION TO COMPUTER

Answer Key

1. (D)	2. (A)	3. (C)	4. (D)	5. (C)	6. (C)	7. (A)	8. (C)	9. (C)	10. (D)
11. (B)	12. (C)	13. (D)	14. (D)	15. (C)	16. (D)	17. (B)	18. (D)	19. (B)	20. (C)

HOTS (ACHIEVERS SECTION)

21. (B)	22. (A)	23. (B)	24. (D)	25. (D)

22. (A)

Device X is a desktop computer, which is not portable, means you cannot carry it wherever you want to. Device Y is a laptop that comes with the touchpad technology as shown below:

23. (B)

Among the given options, only option [B], which is a smartphone is a hand-held device that can be connected to the computer with the help of data cable

2. FUNDAMENTALS OF COMPUTER

Answer Key

1. (D)	2. (B)	3. (D)	4. (D)	5. (B)	6. (B)	7. (A)	8. (A)	9. (C)	10. (A)
11. (A)	12. (B)	13. (C)	14. (B)	15. (C)	16. (B)	17. (A)	18. (B)	19. (B)	20. (D)

HOTS (ACHIEVERS SECTION)

21. (A)	22. (C)	23. (D)	24. (A)	25. (A)

24. (A)

Water acts as an input, and water heater acts as a processor and you get hot water as an output that is heated by the water heater.

3. PARTS OF A COMPUTER

Answer Key

1. (C)	2. (B)	3. (D)	4. (D)	5. (A)	6. (D)	7. (B)	8. (D)	9. (C)	10. (A)
11. (B)	12. (D)	13. (C)	14. (B)	15. (C)	16. (A)	17. (C)	18. (A)	19. (C)	20. (D)

HOTS (ACHIEVERS SECTION)

21. (D)	22. (A)	23. (C)	24. (D)	25. (C)

23. (C)

Option [c] is of Start button, found at the bottom left side of the desktop screen, and rest all the options are the parts of a computer, that you can touch and feel.

24. (D)

The device shown on the left side is of mouse and the one that is show on the right side is of joystick. Joystick is a pointing device, it can be connected to the computer, it is used to give input to the computer and it cannot be used to draw pictures on screen, it is commonly used to play games on computer screen.

25. (C)

We plug this in the power socket to get power for the laptop.

4. USES OF COMPUTER

Answer Key

1. (C)	2. (B)	3. (B)	4. (B)	5. (A)	6. (C)	7. (D)	8. (A)	9. (C)	10. (C)
11. (A)	12. (B)	13. (C)	14. (B)	15. (D)	16. (D)	17. (C)	18. (C)	19. (B)	20. (A)

HOTS (ACHIEVERS SECTION)

21. (A)	22. (D)	23. (D)	24. (B)	25. (D)

5. LEARNING TO USE KEYBOARD

Answer Key

1. (D)	2. (B)	3. (A)	4. (D)	5. (A)	6. (D)	7. (C)	8. (B)	9. (D)	10. (C)
11. (B)	12. (A)	13. (B)	14. (B)	15. (D)	16. (A)	17. (C)	18. (D)	19. (D)	20. (A)

HOTS (ACHIEVERS SECTION)

21. (A)	22. (D)	23. (A)	24. (A)	25. (A)

Answer Key

1. (B)	2. (B)	3. (C)	4. (A)	5. (D)	6. (B)	7. (D)	8. (A)	9. (B)	10. (B)
11. (C)	12. (A)	13. (A)	14. (C)	15. (B)	16. (B)	17. (D)	18. (C)	19. (B)	20. (A)

HOTS (ACHIEVERS SECTION)

21. (C)	22. (B)	23. (B)	24. (A)	25. (A)

7. INTRODUCTION TO MS PAINT

Answer Key

1. (B)	2. (A)	3. (C)	4. (A)	5. (C)	6. (A)	7. (D)	8. (B)	9. (A)	10. (B)
11. (D)	12. (B)	13. (D)	14. (B)	15. (B)	16. (C)	17. (D)	18. (C)	19. (C)	20. (D)

HOTS (ACHIEVERS SECTION)

21. (C)	22. (C)	23. (A)	24. (C)	25. (B)

8. LATEST DEVELOPMENTS IN 'IT'

Answer Key

1. (B)	2. (C)	3. (A)	4. (D)	5. (C)	6. (A)	7. (C)	8. (A)	9. (A)	10. (B)
11. (C)	12. (B)	13. (D)	14. (B)	15. (B)	16. (D)	17. (A)	18. (D)	19. (A)	20. (D)

HOTS (ACHIEVERS SECTION)

21. (B)	22. (A)	23. (D)	24. (D)	25. (A)

23. (D)

The given image is of SD card, known as "Secure Digital" card. It can be read by desktop computers, laptops, smartphones and tablet computers using a special device called card reader.

Answer Key

1. (A)	2. (B)	3. (B)	4. (B)	5. (D)	6. (C)	7. (B)	8. (A)	9. (C)	10. (C)
11. (B)	12. (A)	13. (A)	14. (C)	15. (B)	16. (C)	17. (B)	18. (A)	19. (B)	20. (D)
21. (C)	22. (C)	23. (D)	24. (A)	25. (B)	26. (C)	27. (A)	28. (B)	29. (A)	30. (C)

1. **(A)**
   Add 8 in each number.

2. **(B)**
   Pattern followed in the above series is:
   $80 - 10 = 70 \rightarrow 70 - 15 = 55 \rightarrow 55 - 10 = 45$
   $\rightarrow 45 - 15 = 30$

3. **(B)**
   Except B all the other options have a smaller shape inserted into a bigger shape.

4. **(D)**
   Add 4 to each number. 4.

5. **(C)**
   Option C has six sides whereas shapes in the other options have four sides.

6. **(B)**
   Subtract the even number, respectively:
   $40 - 10 = 30 - 8 = 22$

7. **(A)**
   Each number is multiplied by 3 to get the next number:
   $27 \times 3 = 81 \times 3 = 243$

8. **(C)**
   Terms are multiplied by 2 and 3 alternatively: $2 \times 2 = 4 \times 3 = 12 \times 2 = 24$

9. **(C)**
   As Pen needs Ink to write; similarly Pencil needs Graphite.

10. **(B)**
    States with capital cities

11. **(A)**
    First figure rotates vertically downwards.

12. **(A)**
    As, TABLE $= 20 + 1 + 2 + 12 + 5 = 40$
    Similarly, CHAIR $= 3 + 8 + 1 + 9 + 18 = 39$

13. **(C)**
    As CARROT $= 3 + 1 + 18 + 18 + 15 + 20 = 75$
    Similarly, R A D I S H $= 18 + 1 + 4 + 9 + 19 + 8 = 59$

14. **(B)**
    As S E A $= 19 - 5 - 1 = 13$
    Similarly, Y A K $= 25 - 1 - 11 = 13$

15. **(B)**
    Eraser starts from 1 and ends at 7 cm, so length of the eraser is
    $= 7 \text{ cm} - 1 \text{ cm} = 6 \text{ cm}.$

Answer Key

1. (B)	2. (A)	3. (D)	4. (C)	5. (B)	6. (A)	7. (B)	8. (B)	9. (C)	10. (D)
11. (C)	12. (A)	13. (A)	14. (D)	15. (A)	16. (A)	17. (A)	18. (C)	19. (B)	20. (D)
21. (D)	22. (B)	23. (B)	24. (C)	25. (C)	26. (B)	27. (B)	28. (C)	29. (C)	30. (D)
31. (B)	32. (C)	33. (D)	34. (D)	35. (A)					

SAMPLE OMR ANSWER SHEET

1. STUDENT NAME (IN ENGLISH CAPITAL LETTERS ONLY)

Students must write and darken the respective circles completely using HB Pencil only. Othewise their Answer Sheets will not be evaluated.

PERSONAL DETAILS

2. SCHOOL CODE

3. CLASS

4. SECTION

5. ROLL NO.

6. QUESTION PAPER SET

A ◯ B ◯ C ◯ D ◯

7. MOBILE NUMBER

8. GENDER

MALE ◯

FEMALE ◯

9. STREAM
(Only for Class XI and XII Students)

MATHEMATICS ◯
BIOLOGY ◯
OTHERS ◯

MARK YOUR ANSWERS

1.	A B C D	26.	A B C D
2.	A B C D	27.	A B C D
3.	A B C D	28.	A B C D
4.	A B C D	29.	A B C D
5.	A B C D	30.	A B C D
6.	A B C D	31.	A B C D
7.	A B C D	32.	A B C D
8.	A B C D	33.	A B C D
9.	A B C D	34.	A B C D
10.	A B C D	35.	A B C D
11.	A B C D	36.	A B C D
12.	A B C D	37.	A B C D
13.	A B C D	38.	A B C D
14.	A B C D	39.	A B C D
15.	A B C D	40.	A B C D
16.	A B C D	41.	A B C D
17.	A B C D	42.	A B C D
18.	A B C D	43.	A B C D
19.	A B C D	44.	A B C D
20.	A B C D	45.	A B C D
21.	A B C D	46.	A B C D
22.	A B C D	47.	A B C D
23.	A B C D	48.	A B C D
24.	A B C D	49.	A B C D
25.	A B C D	50.	A B C D

Signature of the Student & Date of Examination

Signature of the Invigilator & Date of Examination

V&S Publishers, F-2/16 Ansari Road, Daryaganj, New Delhi-110002, ☎ 011-23240026-27
✉ info@vspublishers.com, ⊕ www.vspublishers.com